Little Laureates

Heart Of England

Edited by Heather Killingray

First published in Great Britain in 2007 by:
Young Writers
Remus House
Coltsfoot Drive
Peterborough
PE2 9JX
Telephone: 01733 890066
Website: www.youngwriters.co.uk

SB ISBN 978-1 84431 135 4

Foreword

Young Writers was established in 1991 and has been passionately devoted to the promotion of reading and writing in children and young adults ever since. The quest continues today. Young Writers remains as committed to the nurturing of poetic and literary talent as ever.

This year's Young Writers competition has proven as vibrant and dynamic as ever and we are delighted to present a showcase of the best poetry from across the UK and in some cases overseas. Each poem has been selected from a wealth of *Little Laureates* entries before ultimately being published in this, our sixteenth primary school poetry series.

Once again, we have been supremely impressed by the overall quality of the entries we have received. The imagination, energy and creativity which has gone into each young writer's entry made choosing the poems a challenging and often difficult but ultimately hugely rewarding task - the general high standard of the work submitted ensured this opportunity to bring their poetry to a larger appreciative audience.

We sincerely hope you are pleased with this final collection and that you will enjoy *Little Laureates Heart Of England* for many years to come.

Contents

The Poems

Happiness

Happiness is the ball gliding into the back of the net.
Happiness is a choice of tasty puddings at lunchtime.
It tastes likes a soft chocolate cake and smells like a ripe raspberry.
It is the sound of laughter when I play,
Holding hands and football with Daddy.

Happiness plays gentle music on a harp.
Happiness wears orange silks.
Happiness walks briskly in the park.
Happiness is a big circle full of joyful words.

Johnny Day (7)

If You Went Through A Mirror

Imagine if you went through a mirror
The houses would shimmer,
Not like they do today,
What would you say?
I think it would glitter
There would be no dropped litter,
What would you do
If you went through a mirror?

Daisy Flood (8)
Kington Primary School, Kington

My Strange Brother Joe

Up and down the hill I go, with my strange brother Joe
I'm laughing all the way even so I am with my strange brother Joe
I am blowing up balloons today, even though I will be with my
strange brother Joe,
My dad calls my mother Mo, even if he is by my strange brother Joe
I asked my friend if her sister is slow, even though I was with my
strange brother Joe.

Kate Bree (7)
Kington Primary School, Kington

Robin Hood

Robin Hood and his group
Were having a bowl of soup
Having a great big feast
When along came a big beast.

Robin shot an arrow
It hit a marrow
Fell on the beast's head
And then it was dead.

It was spinning round and round
As it fell to the ground,
They carried on with the feast
As they cooked the big, big beast.

First they skinned the beast
And took off all its hair.
They stuck the poor beast on a stick
Then Little John kicked a poor harmless chick.

The sheriff watching them run
As he ate an iced bun.

They stuffed their faces
And ran to their secret bases.
With arms full of money
And jars full of honey.

Sam Stevens (9)
Mordiford CE Primary School, Mordiford Hereford

My Friend

My friend, my friend, weird as can be
She's going funny and so is me
Funny Abbi, funny Abbi, she likes dogs
And so do we
Pink, pink, she likes pink
Witches, witches scary things . . .

Cha Prosser (9)
Mordiford CE Primary School, Mordiford Hereford

Maud And The Mordiford Dragon

There was once a girl called Maud,
Who was walking out in the wood.
She stumbled upon a baby dragon,
Maud thought it would be good.

Her wish was shattered in the next few weeks,
The dragon was a killer
He'd eaten up the pub's assistant,
And the local miller.

The villagers got together
They needed to be rid of this beast.
But they had no such luck,
For all the dragon wanted was a hearty feast.

Then a villager had a plan
It was an idea so great,
But if it went the slightest bit wrong,
He'd meet with a terrible fate.

He hid inside a wooden barrel,
He watched go by a cart,
And when the dragon approached him,
He leapt up and shot at its heart.

The dragon let out a piteous howl,
And uttered out his last fatal breath,
Killing the villager dead,
But at the same time he met with his death.

The dragon is remembered
As something nasty and foul,
And all the villagers cheered,
As he let out his last howl.

So that is the story,
The end of his life.

Rosie Cox (9)
Mordiford CE Primary School, Mordiford Hereford

No Poem In My Mind

There's no poem in my mind
My mind is blank
No poem can I find
I can't think of a rhyme
My mind's a blur
My mind has stopped
It's dead, it's gone,
All I can think of is a slur.
What can I write?
What can it be about?
What shall I put down?
A ball, a book or a pig's snout
We've got a rhyming dictionary,
But there's nothing that I can write,
Nothing that will suit me,
Nothing that catches my sight,
But oh well I can write about nothing.

Lauren Hart (9)
Mordiford CE Primary School, Mordiford Hereford

Going To Bed

Going to bed this night
There's monsters all about
I'm all curled in bed in fright
Witches lurk about outside.

All the ghosts are coming towards you
Some are waving swords
Some are shouting boo
I'm quivering like mad.

They're way too loud
I can't ignore them,
'Night,' the werewolf howled
And they all go away.

Kate Greenow (9)
Mordiford CE Primary School, Mordiford Hereford

The Horse That I Love

I put the saddle on her back,
Because *clip-clop, clip-clop,* we're going on a hack.
I place the bridle on her face,
And we set off at a smashing pace!

We started at a fast canter,
I think we were going as fast as Santa!
We were riding past great big fir trees,
Until we bumped into a swarm of huge angry bees.

My horse was tired,
So we rode to my gate, which was weird.
I put her in her little stable,
And guess who came out to greet me,
But my sis, Mable!

I woke up to a wonderful new day,
And got up out of the bed to give my horse some hay.
I decided to have a game,
Oh, I remember it's Flossy, that's her name!

Lydia Glendinning (10)
Mordiford CE Primary School, Mordiford Hereford

My Dream

My dream is to play for Man U alongside Giggs
Who can supply a strong solid kick
On the side of the pitch.

My dream is to play for Man U and win the UEFA Cup
And I might be the first to lift it up.

My dream is to play for Man U and win the Carling Cup
Reading have been tough so far
But we'll beat them soon enough.

At the moment I play at Ledbury, a town in Herefordshire
I play on the wing and I tackle hard
So other players have some fear.

Eliot Broadbridge (9)
Mordiford CE Primary School, Mordiford Hereford

The City Of Lo-Yang

I climb to the ridge of Pei-Mang mountain,
And look down at the city of Lo-Yang
In Lo-Yang how tremendously loud it is
Palaces and houses drawing the eye
Streams of smoke shooting up to the sky
Young and old alike
Little kids on their trikes.

Fields neatly ploughed
And the noise is deafeningly loud
I can't turn away
I just let my eyes stray
Over the bright streets
And as the sheep behind me bleats
I dream of what I soon will see
Empty streets and a dead tree
The sad, the sorry and the empty.

Charlotte Hart (11)
Mordiford CE Primary School, Mordiford Hereford

A Superhero Sends A Letter Home

Dear Mum,
Things have been going excellent lately.
My super powers are working greatly.
Police aren't doing any work.
The press are going berserk.
Every villain in the town
Wants my shiny, gleaming crown.
I've got these people in the bag
I'm getting ladies like I'm playing tag.
I take my suit to *my* launderette
They haven't managed to shrink it yet.
So as you can see,
It's good for me.
From your little superhero
Flame Slayer!

Mikey Hollis (11)
Mordiford CE Primary School, Mordiford Hereford

A Superhero Sends A Letter Home

Dear Family,
I've just got to tell you something and you might freak out,
The thing is I've got secret powers please don't shout,
I cannot tell you just how, but let's say I fell,
Don't worry I am well.

I woke up this morning covered in fur,
When I tried to talk, it came out like a purr,
My fingernails had turned to claws,
And I was walking on all fours.

I still can't believe it now,
Because I didn't know how,
I am back to normal
And I am living in Cornwall.

But occasionally I still miaow.

Anya Birch (10)
Mordiford CE Primary School, Mordiford Hereford

Me

My name's Leo,
Hazelnut hair,
I'm up for a dare,
Loves footy,
Play for greyhound
Undefeated for many years 1, 2, 3
Got loads of mates,
They're all greats
Green eyes,
Go to Mordiford School
It rules!
Loves PE,
Hate DT
That's the sum up of me!

Leo Bristow (11)
Mordiford CE Primary School, Mordiford Hereford

Splish, Splash, Splosh

Bibble, bobble, splish, splash, splosh
Make this potion turn into dosh.

Chuck some things
In a pot
There is plenty of stuff
I'll use the lot.

Bibble, bobble, splish, splash, splosh
Make this potion turn into dosh.

I'll buy a broomstick
I'll buy a wand
I'll buy a lair
I'll buy a pond.

Bibble, bobble, splish, splash, splosh
Please make this potion turn into dosh.

The money will all be mine
I won't donate any of it
The money will be in my palm
And everyone will have a fit.

Bibble, bobble, splish, splash, splosh
Please make this potion turn into dosh.

I'll be rich, filthy rich
I'll swim in my money
They will all fall for it
And that will be funny
Hahahahaha

Bibble, bobble, splish, splash, splosh
Please make this potion turn into dosh.

Rhys Cooper (10)
Mordiford CE Primary School, Mordiford Hereford

The Forever Changing Seasons

Winter is cold,
Winter has snow,
Winter is really old,
And all the rivers really start to flow.

Spring is warm,
Spring is tame,
And bees start to swarm
Then they make the sheep go lame.

Autumn makes the leaves fall off the trees,
Autumn makes the lambs start to grow,
But it makes me sneeze,
And it makes the branches of the trees really go low.

Summer is time to harvest the corn,
It is time to cut the grass,
On the garden lawn,
But don't forget your bus pass.

Oliver Powell (9)
Mordiford CE Primary School, Mordiford Hereford

My Poem Is Too Big For My Paper!

What can I do, my poem is too long?
The teacher might say, 'That's all wrong.'
I'm shrieking, I'm worrying,
I'm scurrying and scurrying.
What can I do, my poem is too big for my paper?
I wish I had a special taper,
He or she would tape it all up,
I'm just so fed up.

Shall I turn the page?
Shall I start a newspaper?
Shall I tell the teacher?
I just want to caper,
I'm running out, can I make it?
I get smaller and smaller and . . .

Jacob Broadbridge (9)
Mordiford CE Primary School, Mordiford Hereford

Harvest Poem

I asked a girl who cannot see,
What is colour like?

Yellow's for the sun
Warm and bright

Blue is for the wind
Cold in the night.

Green is for the grass
Waving in the breeze

Grey is for the smoke
That makes you cough and sneeze.

Silver is for a dream
That stays with you forever

Gold is for your friends
As you always play together.

Black is what everything looks to me.

Emily Greenow (10)
Mordiford CE Primary School, Mordiford Hereford

Beaming Island

The golden sand
Stretches before you.

The crystal-blue sea
Crashing on the gleaming soft sand
While the glowing sun beams down on the beach.

Where the turtle
Are roaming about.

When the towering palm tree
Swaying in the breeze
And soothe you into relaxation.

Sophie Fortey (11)
Mordiford CE Primary School, Mordiford Hereford

Sparklers

Sparklers in the night
They shimmer and glow
The night flies
As my birthday comes and goes.

Rockets blaze as they explode
They let out smoke
As they fly over to the road.

Charlotte Oakley (9)
Mordiford CE Primary School, Mordiford Hereford

Bikers

Biker's inns and biker's gear
Watch out they have no fear
They're big and scary
Also hairy
Skulls and flames
They cannot be trained
Harleys and KTMs
They are the biker men.

Owen Rogers (10)
Mordiford CE Primary School, Mordiford Hereford

Happy

Happy is yellow
Happy smells fresh
Happy tastes sweet
Happy sounds joyful
Happy feels special
Happy lives everywhere.

Mary Whitting (9)
Mordiford CE Primary School, Mordiford Hereford

Life Is A Poem

Life is a poem with giggles along the way.
Dancing dragons and leaping lizards jumping through the sky . . .
Don't make me remember those cheeky koalas saying hello and hi.
Don't forget as we flow to take a peep down below.

Is it frogs with bright yellow polka dots
Or kangaroos with chickenpox
Or fluffy kittens wearing socks?

Have you seen the purple bear
Hanging in its purple lair?

Are you writing about a roaring mouse
Sneaking in your empty house

Or maybe just a poem with giggles along the way?

Victoria Gill
St Anne's Catholic Primary School, Stafford

Dog Party

Please come to my dog party,
We'll have a good time,
I'll tell Mum that you're coming,
It starts at nine.

We might have a pillow fight,
A Snack-a-Jack or two,
The dogs will have water,
And meat vindaloo.

And then in the morning,
We will cuddle up in bed,
And after we wake up,
We'll have home-made jam and bread.

Amy Harwood (9)
St Anne's Catholic Primary School, Stafford

Weather Goes Mad

One day there was biting wind,
It was stormy and cloudy,
Forecaster is not happy,
He is a lovely chappy,
But sometimes he can be yappy.
He saw a boy playing with his toy,
The wind blew it out of his hand,
And it smashed on the ground,
The forecaster went outside
Thunder roared, lightning cracked
It rained and rained.
He wished he had his coat,
Biting winds came and knocked him down
That was the end of the biting wind.

Casey McDonnell (9)
St Anne's Catholic Primary School, Stafford

Can You Be My Friend?

Can you be my friend?
If you are I will:
Read with you,
Play with you,
Have lots of fun with you.

We'll laugh, we'll cry
We'll be friends until we die,
If only you'll be my friend.

Friends are for life,
But we must make sure we never fight,
Because that's just not right
Can you be my friend?

Laura Connaughton
St Anne's Catholic Primary School, Stafford

All About Wrestling

I want to have a picnic with Sabu,
I'll try to get some cranberry juice too,
You can bring a chair, roar like a bear,
But I don't care, because I'm going to beat you.

I want to fight John Cena,
But definitely in the arena,
Put me through a table, squash me like a baked potato,
But I don't care, because I'll still beat you.

I'll play with Sandman,
Smash a beer can,
Hit somebody over the head with a frying pan,
But I don't care, I'll still beat you.

I'll sing with Tommy Dreamer,
He just gets meaner and meaner,
Throw me off a ladder, hit me with a chair,
But I don't care, I'll still beat you . . .

. . . oh by the way, stay away from Umaga, or he'll make you pay!

James Curtin (10)
St Anne's Catholic Primary School, Stafford

Golden Sand

Golden sand, glitters and glows,
And in the night it really shows.
Dancing fairies skipping along,
Singing their sweet melody song.

Happy memories made with fun,
Underneath the hot bright sun,
Love and laughter, times we spent,
Never realising how much they meant.

In years to come they will be
Our most precious treasure,
Leaving us with memories beyond, any other measure.

Chelsea Merricks (8)
St Anne's Catholic Primary School, Stafford

Electric Floor Polisher

Our electric floor polisher,
Sucks up rather too much stuff,
It's swallowed my brother's dead fish,
And Mum's seven-year-old brush.

My dad's underwear,
My sister's forty-two inch TV,
My cousin's floppy rag doll,
And knitting needles three!

A Pink Floyd poster,
A mouldy cup of tea,
My DVDs and more,
You really wouldn't believe.

Our electric floor polisher,
Must have had a really *bad* brand,
I really think we should,
Start doing it by hand!

Katie Murray (9)
St Anne's Catholic Primary School, Stafford

I Am A Fairy's Child

Dancing on leaves singing songs,
Whistling with our little tongues
I was born with fairy friends
Our relationship never ends
We always glow in the night,
It truly is a beautiful sight,
We sleep on flower petals
That's where we normally settle,
We take care of each other
And will always love our fairy mother
As we watch the setting sun
A fairy's child is so much fun.

Danielle Gray
St Anne's Catholic Primary School, Stafford

Stars

At night-time the stars glow,
How far away we do not know.
Shooting across the deep black sky,
Never stopping, continuing to fly!

I see the stars brightly shine,
And pretend that they are all mine.
They light up the dark at night,
So no one ever gets a fright.

They glitter like shining gold,
They've been here for years they must be so old.
Some get tired and fall from the sky,
They want a rest, they don't want to fly!

Some stars shoot past the moon,
But don't worry they will be back soon.
I want to spread my wings and fly,
Like those shiny stars in the sky.

Abi Martin (10)
St Anne's Catholic Primary School, Stafford

Girls

Tough girls, rough girls
Sad girls, mad girls
Nice girls, spice girls
Girly girls, curly girls
Naughty girls, sporty girls
That's about enough girls.

Sophie Withers (9)
St Anne's Catholic Primary School, Stafford

Back To Work

As soon as I get home from work,
My wife says to me,
'Had a nice day at work
Did Raymond go to sleep?'
I had my tea, then sat down
Why is work so important?
I thought with a frown.

I went out for my evening stroll,
All my employees out too,
'Hi Boss,' they shout,
Katie, Ben and my mate Sue!
'Hi,' I shout back,
As I pull out my midnight snack.

Back to work tomorrow,
I thought as I lay in my bed
And I went to sleep
With my soft ted.

Amy Pearson (9)
St Anne's Catholic Primary School, Stafford

I'm Scared Of . . .

Slimy strange worms with germs,
I'm scared of balloons with cartoons on them,
I'm scared of old men who act like they're ten,
I'm scared of my barmy brother,
But I'm glad now he's gone to his den,
I'm scared of the hen that ate my friend Ben,
I'm scared of a scary puppet but people just say that it's a Muppet,
I'm scared of the dark but so is my friend Clark,
The thing I'm most scared of is my head teacher's big fat creature,
(Who hides in our toilets).

Daniel Ferguson (10)
St Anne's Catholic Primary School, Stafford

It's Party Time!

P resents, treats and ice cream
A birthday wishing dream
R eady for my friends to come
T he birthday cake is almost done
Y our birthday, it's your birthday!

T elevision, calling out names
I win lots of games
M ums and dads drinking beer
E verybody's here.

Emma Nicholls (9)
St Anne's Catholic Primary School, Stafford

A Birthday Present

A birthday present,
A decent pheasant,

A bright red ribbon,
A closet that's forbidden,

A new cuddly toy,
A cute baby girl or boy,

A snappy crocodile,
A snazzy flip-top mobile,

A colourful fox,
What's this a pair of socks?

Sophie Gordon (9)
St Anne's Catholic Primary School, Stafford

Third Time Fergy

'Third Time Fergy'
Gets everything the third time
Whether it's answers or goals
Or falling in holes.

Once in a football match
When his team were losing 3-2.
When their striker caught the flu
'Third Time Fergy' knew just what to do.

He sped down the pitch at a terrific pace
Almost like he was in a race
Twice he had a chance to shoot
He was feeling lucky with his right boot.

So then it came the third attempt
To the back of the net, the ball it went
Way to go 'Third Time Fergy', we have won again.

Joe Hallows (10)
St Anne's Catholic Primary School, Stafford

A Scared Dragon

Everyone thinks a dragon
Is strong and fierce
And attacks knights
But they are nice
And very shy and
Quiet and helpful
So you help them
And you might
Have a surprise.

Joshua Nicholls (10)
St Anne's Catholic Primary School, Stafford

The River

From a small trickle, a mere stream,
Gentle as it may seem
Pouring down the countryside, gathering speed
A drill - smashing its path across the once dry land.
Twisting, turning, whirling, churning
Trying to find its way to the vast ocean.
It comes across a cliff it cannot get through,
What does it do?
Gallons of water cascading over the rocks.
Other rivers join to continue on their journey.
Gallons of water going faster than any creature.
Finally it smashes into the sea.
So if I were you, I would never underestimate a stream.

Jack Doyle (11)
St Francis Xavier's RC Primary School, Hereford

The River

Crystal clear
Fast and slow
Oh so near
Get ready to go.

Go quite fast
It's getting wide
Get there first
We'll miss the tide.

Come on now a few more miles
Under the bridge and out of the tiles.

I think we're there
I can't see the river
The sea is big
It makes me shiver.

Daniel Bythell (11)
St Francis Xavier's RC Primary School, Hereford

What Am I?

Trickling over the soft earth,
Nothing in my way.
Keeping lots of things alive,
What am I?

You can sail on me,
And I'll take you for a ride,
Down towards the sea I head,
What am I?

My skin shall glisten like a star,
While I sway in the moonlight,
I am the prettiest of every known thing,
What am I?

I am the river who invades the land,
I give life to certain things,
I'm the river of life.

Sophie Orr (10)
St Francis Xavier's RC Primary School, Hereford

The River

The thrashing river passed by.
Hurry past the river clashing on the rocks.
Escaping through the misty lands.
Rippling through the water swish,
Swish it goes.
Invading through the lands a powerful swirling gush.
Varied inside, she swims along.
Eager to swish and sway around the trickling waters.
Round and round the river goes
Swishing and swaying and rapidly flows.

Andrew Ling (10)
St Francis Xavier's RC Primary School, Hereford

When My Mum Gives Me A Hug

Everyone rejoice and be happy
Today is the day of celebration
For the whole world spins around me
When my mum smiles.

The world is full of gladness
That fills them up with joy
Let us dance and be happy
When my mum sings.

The world is dark and full of sadness
Only with a pinch of joy
There is nothing more in the world
When my mum cries.

Leah Cottrell (9)
St Francis Xavier's RC Primary School, Hereford

When My . . .

When my best friend plays with me
It makes me as happy as happy can be.

When my sister makes me giggle
She does it by tickling me
And it makes me all wriggly.

When my mum gives me a hug
I feel as warm as hot soup in a mug.

When my teacher says, 'Well done'
I feel proud indeed
I feel as proud as a knight
Riding a trusty steed.

Will Aston (8)
St Francis Xavier's RC Primary School, Hereford

The River

I lay down on the banks,
I gently lower my hand into the water,
It is cold to the touch.
I let my hand do as it pleases,
Letting the water carry it away.

The water is so clear,
Crystal clear,
I pick up a stone
Dripping wet from the bottom of the riverbed,
I gently rub it with my thumb,
Then place it back in the water
And watch it slowly sink.

I sit up
Looking at the water gushing past me
And I wonder,
How did something so small,
Turn into something so amazing
Swirling and whirling,
Glimmering and shimmering.

But then I wonder,
Is it lonely?
There is only one river,
Flowing past me,
But when it joins the sea again,
Maybe it is happy.

But I don't worry anymore,
Because it's so beautiful
You seem to forget all your troubles
And you seem to feel peaceful,
Once again.

I lay down on the banks,
Looking down at the river,
As it rushes past me,
I turn over and just lie there,
Motionless.

Ellie Long (11)
St Francis Xavier's RC Primary School, Hereford

The River

The gleeful river starts,
Trickling down from the tops of the mountains,
Meandering from side to side,
Slithering along just like a snake,
Shaping its path as it goes.

Suddenly gathering speed,
Faster, faster, *swerving, curving*
Turning into a cheetah chasing its prey,
Then from out of nowhere,
Whoosh,
It plummets over the jagged walls,
Into the pool, the plunge pool,
Crashing, splashing, bashing.

Eroding, destroying, gathering,
Whilst going past,
Invading the dry green land,
Slowing down to the pace of a snail,
Just to watch the animals rushing past.

Adventurously cascading,
Proudly flowing along,
Then comes a whirling whirlpool,
The river's worst enemy,
It creates an evil look,
Then charges straight at it,
Smashing it and crushing it into small pieces.

Along come the rapids,
The river rides along the rapids,
Like a person riding a horse,
Then far in the distance,
It looks like the vicious sea,
The river slows down immediately,
Getting scared but just, just,
Can't stop *woooaaahh*
It's the sea.

But it doesn't stop there,
Oh no,
The river will always be there,
Starting as a trickle,
Ending as an uncontrollable gush of water.

Kathryn Morison (11)
St Francis Xavier's RC Primary School, Hereford

The River

Drip, drip, drip
Trickle, trickle, trickle
A river is born.

Cut, cut, cut,
Drill, drill, drill,
The river grows.

Down, down, down
Plunge, plunge, plunge
It takes its first dive.

Faster, faster, faster
Quicker, quicker, quicker
The river is a rapid.

Splash, splash, splash
Crash, crash, crash
The river plays with the rocks.

Twisting, twisting, twisting
Turning, turning, turning
The river meanders like a snake.

Bigger, bigger, bigger
Wider, wider, wider
Finally the sea, the river is now grown up.

Warren Parker (11)
St Francis Xavier's RC Primary School, Hereford

When My Mum . . .

When my mum gives me a cuddle
I feel good inside
When my mum shouts at me
I feel bad inside
When my mum talks to me
I feel weird inside
When my mum ignores me
I feel annoyed inside.

When my dad . . .
When my dad plays with me
I feel happy inside
When my dad buys Amy presents
I feel left out inside
When my dad reads me stories
I feel calm inside
When my dad's team wins against Arsenal
I feel disappointed inside.

When my mum and dad take me on holiday
I feel loved inside!

Ben Sadler (9)
St Francis Xavier's RC Primary School, Hereford

The Snow

It reflects
Shovels scooping up the snow,
'That's heavy.'
People driving cars - 3, 2, 1, *crash!*
Children sledging on the hillside - splat!
Ice skaters skating, figures of eight.
Planes de-iced on the runway, 'It's cold out here!'
Farm animals in their barns - warm and dry.

Niamh Callaghan (7)
St Leonard's CE (VC) First School, Dunston

The Wind

The wind runs over you like a stampede.
It flies through the garden
Pulling out the weeds.
Too strong it brings disasters.
Storm chasers have to be masters.
It blows off roof tiles
And carries people for miles.
Cars do terrible skids,
They knock over kids.
You knock over ships that's your motion
And send all the crew to the bottom of the ocean.
If you know what you did
You wouldn't make that car do a terrible skid!
We all call you Mister
Wwwwiiinnnddd!

Chris Heffernan (8)
St Leonard's CE (VC) First School, Dunston

Cat In The Window

Cat in the window what do you see?
Cloud, wind, leaves, a squirrel in a tree.
The daffodils shivering in a January breeze,
A cloud rolling by in a frost-bitten sky.

Jazmine Harvey (7)
St Leonard's CE (VC) First School, Dunston

The Snow

It reflects
Sam and Cam having snowball fights
Snowballs soft and cold on my back
My cheeks are warm
But my feet are cold.

Callum Price (7)
St Leonard's CE (VC) First School, Dunston

Snow Falling

It reflects
A big red car going really slow.
Children sledging on the highest hill.
The schools closing, playgrounds covered.
The small pony standing freezing cold.
Big snowmen with carrot noses.
Happy dogs licking and eating snow.

Natalie Lippitt (8)
St Leonard's CE (VC) First School, Dunston

The Snow

It reflects trees covered with snow
Gritters gritting the road
Cars slowing down
Trains being delayed
Airports closed
People brushing snow off their driveways
People walking in the freezing snow
Schools closed, people at home by their fires.

Lewis Burton (8)
St Leonard's CE (VC) First School, Dunston

Snow Falling

It reflects
Children playing on great white slopes
Flimsy toboggans jumping and flying
Callum throwing snowballs at his mum
Clouds spitting snow
Frozen cars stuck in the snow
The yellow snowplough scooping it up.

Cameron Campbell (7)
St Leonard's CE (VC) First School, Dunston

The Snow

It reflects
Bright yellow, snow ploughs, pushing the hard snow
Cars won't start, engines frozen.
Sam's making the world's biggest snowman
Callum laughing as he falls over.
Dad scraping the snow from the window.
People tobogganing.

Sam Myatt (8)
St Leonard's CE (VC) First School, Dunston

The Snow

It reflects
Noisy children playing on their sledges catching snow
Flakes in their mouths, making snowmen, having a good time.
Schools are closed, people sitting by the fire in their houses,
keeping warm.

Emily Hampton (8)
St Leonard's CE (VC) First School, Dunston

Winter

The snow is a cheetah
Charging in from nowhere.
The snow is a cheetah
Dangerous, detached and destructive.

His temper's like a whirlwind
Affecting all around
Paralysing and numbing,
All in its path.

Sadie Lewis (11)
St Patrick's RC Primary School, Stafford

Predator

The snow is a cobra
Silently, spitefully swallowing his prey
Swiftly sabotages his world . . .
Vicious and victorious
Prey versus predator, sun versus snow.

Monique Senior (10)
St Patrick's RC Primary School, Stafford

I Wish

I wish I was a footballer with lots of cash
I wish I was a race car driver that is very funny
I wish I played football out in the day that is sunny
I wish I had a black bunny.

I wish I had a PlayStation 3
I wish my grandad wasn't fifty
I wish I had a talking tree
I wish my brother was sixty.

I wish I had a lolly
I wish I had a sister
I wish my friend was jolly
I wish no one left litter.

Denzel Effiom (9)
St Patrick's RC Primary School, Stafford

Snow

The snow is a sabotaging shark
Huge and hungry for its pitiful prey
Swimming like a stealthy, silent submarine,
Spreading a white blanket,
Of doom over the town.

Alex Wainwright (10)
St Patrick's RC Primary School, Stafford

Snow

The snow is a mouse
Creeping through your street.
It has no intention of stopping,
Gnawing at all it can see.
When morning comes, snow is gone,
And green once more rules the Earth
But crumbs of snow still remain.

Tom Gibson (11)
St Patrick's RC Primary School, Stafford

Owl Snow

Like an owl, the snow gracefully flutters down,
Silent and spiteful,
Shrivelling flowers forbidden to grow
Cold car coughs
Snow-coated plains spreading far and wide
Dawn arrives
Snow flies away
Grass has come now
To stay!

Derek Effiom (11)
St Patrick's RC Primary School, Stafford

Fox

The snow is a fox
Creeping slyly, silently
Towards its prey . . .
It gnaws at your fingers
Spitting them out like helpless
Bones from a
Broken body.

Maddie Cooper (10)
St Patrick's RC Primary School, Stafford

Mugs Of Bugs

Inside the magic room I saw . . .
Mugs of bugs
Loads of toads
Jars of stars
Bins of pins
Box of socks
Boats of coats
Dish of fish
Pools of jewels
Chests of vests
Pockets of lockets
Cups of pups
Crates of plates
Vans of pans
Jars of cars
Beds of heads.

Chloe Buckingham (8)
St Patrick's RC Primary School, Stafford

I Wish

I wish I had a puppy
I wish the pipes wouldn't jingle
I wish my clothes weren't muddy
I wish more people would mingle.

I wish I had an Xbox 360
I wish I was famous
I wish my sister wasn't so trixy
I wish my life was completely shameless.

I wish I worked as a clown
I wish I had a tan
I wish my room was brown
I wish my brother wasn't a man
I wish, I wish, I wish, I wish.

Erin Sweeney (9)
St Patrick's RC Primary School, Stafford

I Wish

I wish I was taller
I wish I was funny
I wish everyone was smaller
I wish I smelt like honey.

I wish I had lots of jewels
I wish I would never die
I wish there was no rules
I wish I could fly.

I wish I had curly hair
I wish I never went to the loo
I wish there was no such thing as a bear
I wish I was . . .
You!

Abbie Meddings (8)
St Patrick's RC Primary School, Stafford

I Saw . . .

I saw a lion walking on a road
I saw a genie bringing to life a toad
I saw a pretty mermaid walking on land
I saw a yellow duck swiming in sand
I saw an orange starfish sitting in a box
I saw a flying purple fox
I saw a dog walking on his hind legs
I saw a sheep hanging her washing up with pegs
I saw an elf with knobbly knees
I saw a hummingbird eating green beans
I saw a pink river Nile
I saw a sheep who gave me a smile
I saw a cow flying his kite
I thought to myself *what a wonderful sight.*

Mollie Edensor (9)
St Patrick's RC Primary School, Stafford

Winter Is A Jeweller

Winter is a jeweller,
Turning puddles into mirrors
And raindrops into diamonds
And berries into rubies.
Glittering and sparkling and shining
The world looks like a shop window
That's the season to be happy and giving presents.

Louise Whibley (8)
St Patrick's RC Primary School, Stafford

I Saw . . .

I saw a witch drinking loads of beer
I saw a ghost hovering in fear
I saw a man turning into a toad
I saw a lion walking on the road
I saw a van talking too loud
I saw a vest walking through a crowd
I saw a man looking for his van
I saw a boy looking for a pan.

Kieran Washington (9)
St Patrick's RC Primary School, Stafford

Snow

The snow is an eagle
It soars gracefully in the air
Then dives swiftly to the ground, settles
And covers its prey
Soon to return to its home again.

Grace Poole (11)
St Patrick's RC Primary School, Stafford

Mugs Of Bugs

Mugs of bugs
Loads of toads
Jars of stars
Bins of pins
Box of socks
Boats of coats
Dish of fish
Pools of jewels
Chest of vets
Pockets of lockets
Beds of heads
Rooms of brooms
Cups of pups
Packs of snacks
Crates of plates.

Alexandra Price (9)
St Patrick's RC Primary School, Stafford

I Wish

I wish I was a lolly
I wish I had long hair
I wish I had a dolly
I wish I was the mayor.

I wish I could throw a ball
I wish my dad could stay at home
I wish I was quite tall
I wish I had a comb.

I wish I had another brother
I wish I was in care
I wish I could take cover
I wish I liked pears!

Megan Garnett (9)
St Patrick's RC Primary School, Stafford

I Saw . . .

I saw a peacock black and white
I saw a cloud blue in the night
I saw a lion on the road
I saw a magician making a toad
I saw a dragon eating a snail
I saw a wizard looking pale
I saw a witch looking for a maid
I saw a giant in the parade
I saw a troll with a tape fall
I saw an elf to trace
I saw a sea horse in the sea
I saw a fairy, we're best friends you and me.

Lewis Charlesworth (9)
St Patrick's RC Primary School, Stafford

I Saw A Mermaid

I saw a mermaid with a glittering tail,
I saw a flying pig fetching the mail,
I saw a giant talking to himself,
I saw Santa giving jam to his elves,
I saw a clown with a big red nose,
I saw a fairy with dainty little toes,
I saw a grizzly bear washing his clothes,
I saw a little girl sniffing a rose,
I saw the King and I saw the Queen,
I saw a roadrunner that's what I've seen,
I saw all these things with my own two eyes!
But I have to go now before the sun starts to rise.

Erin Kiely (8)
St Patrick's RC Primary School, Stafford

I Saw A . . .

I saw a flying pig flying in the air
I saw a pink troll just over there
I saw a gold lion rolling in the snow
I saw a small dragon flying very low
I saw a calendar talking to his friend
I saw a unicorn, he said the world will never end.
I saw a small pheasant crawling on the ground,
I saw a big elf who could not hear a sound.
I saw a chocolate river floating in the sky,
I saw a peacock with a sore thigh.
I saw all these things before I went to bed,
I saw all these things because they're in my head.

Megan Wright (8)
St Patrick's RC Primary School, Stafford

I Saw A Dragon

I saw a dragon breathing snow,
I saw an elf with a big toe,
I saw a giant with a big shoe,
I saw a ballerina with a tutu,
I saw a toad all on his own,
I saw a giant who likes to groan,
I saw a fairy in the sky,
I saw a birdy way up high,
I saw a lion roaring very loud,
I saw a monkey standing very proud,
I saw this with my very own eyes,
Now the sun is beginning to rise.

Angel Allsop (9)
St Patrick's RC Primary School, Stafford

I Saw A . . .

I saw a money tree walking up to me
I saw a gentle bird flutter down to my knee
I saw a diamond dazzling like a star
I saw a ruby, red in a jar
I saw a gold, bright, yellow chest
I saw a puppy that had to go to the vets
I saw a coat that had no pockets
I saw a secret passage that lead to a rocket
I saw a giant rabbit hopping all around
I saw a mouse carrying ten pounds
I saw a stripy goat jumping up and down
I saw a spotty frog wearing a crown.

Lauren Devlin (9)
St Patrick's RC Primary School, Stafford

I Saw . . .

I saw a horse with a tail like a streaming river
I saw an apple tree give a great shiver
I saw a pig up in the sky
I saw a turtle up up high
I saw a star down on the ground
I saw a trumpet that did not make a sound
I saw a duck that swam in the sea
I saw a house without a key
I saw a bird in a well
I saw a mermaid in a shell
I saw the night come to a sudden close
As I saw the morning sun rose.

Megan Challinor (8)
St Patrick's RC Primary School, Stafford

Something Inside So Strong

(Inspired by the song 'Something Inside So Strong' by Labi Siffre)

I know that I can force it
Cos if I don't it will be worse,
No there's something inside so strong
Oh something that's so strong.

People and others
When they insist we are just no good,
Well I know better,
Just look at them real hard and say,
I'll always make it anyway.

Something inside so strong
I know that I can face it
Cos if I don't it will be worse,
No there's something inside so strong
Oh something that's so strong.

People and others,
When they insist we are no good,
Well I know better,
Just look at them real hard and say
I'll always make it anyway.

Larissa Evans (11)
Seabridge Primary School, Newcastle-under-Lyme

Spiders

The big, hairy spider came out from behind the telly,
I had an awful feeling in my belly.
What if it crawled up inside my trouser leg
Or made its way into my bed?
Those big, long legs and hairy body
Make me nervous, scared and have a dodgy tummy.
I beg my mum to try and catch it.
Hairy spiders, I just can't *hack it!*

Liam Wilson (9)
Seabridge Primary School, Newcastle-under-Lyme

Wasps!

They drive me buzzing crazy
When they're buzzing round my head
I find them quite lazy
When they're sleeping in their bed.

But when they awake from their sleeping heads
I drip with anxious sweat
That I'm dreading what's going to happen next
Their tail starts to wiggle and
Their buzz gets even louder.

I know what's going to happen next,
I try to run but their sting is too powerful,
I tremble a bit, I just can't take it anymore.

A tear runs down my cheek, but I quickly wipe it away
Then in my loudest voice I scream,
'Wasps go away I've had enough.'

This sends the black and yellowed uniformed wasps
Racing towards me
But I knew I'd had enough
So I got the whopping fly splatter
And launched at them with a *splat!*

Tamika Williamson (10)
Seabridge Primary School, Newcastle-under-Lyme

My Haikus

Snow
Snow can be awesome
Making snowmen or sledging
Yippee I love snow.

Daffodils
Daffodils are tall
They are slender and yellow
They sway in the breeze.

Alex Martin (11)
Seabridge Primary School, Newcastle-under-Lyme

Sometimes I Get It Wrong

(Inspired by the song 'Something Inside So Strong' by Labi Siffre)

No matter the weather, I'll work hard,
The stronger I will come.
Harder the race; the faster I run -
The calmer I will come.
You can be my friend;
New friend and old friend will be there with me,
No matter you see.

Sometimes I get it wrong,
I'll try my best all the time.
Tho' I panic, I'll do it;
Oh on, sometimes I get it wrong,
Oh, oh, oh, oh, oh, sometimes I get it wrong.

The more I think about the future
The harder I will try.
The trip will be fun for me and you
We will enjoy it there
Camping with my friends -
Higher the care, the stronger I will come;
No matter which way.
Sometimes I get it wrong . . .

Lauren Titley (11)
Seabridge Primary School, Newcastle-under-Lyme

Haikus

Books
Reading very fun
You can learn lots of good words
The end of the book.

Sports
Football is sporty
Kick a ball into the goal
Now take a free kick.

Jordan Tomkins (11)
Seabridge Primary School, Newcastle-under-Lyme

Leg Spinner's Song

(Inspired by the song 'Something Inside So Strong' by Labi Siffre)

The quicker you bowl your leg spin bowl,
The wider it becomes,
The harder you bowl your leg spin bowl
The faster it will run.
You can't tell me,
How my bowling should be:
No matter cos . . . there's

Something inside so strong,
I know that I can bowl it.
Though you are teaching me wrong, so wrong
You thought that my spin was wrong, oh no!
I know that I can spin it
But you're teaching me wrong, so wrong.

The more you say my spin is bad
The more you make me mad.
You hide behind your coaching ways
All I do is count the days,
Until I find you;

My overs will blind you
And my game will shine so brightly
It will astound you;
No matter . . . cos there's

Here comes the flipper
Sliding down the track, hits the middle stump and he's out.
People screaming down my ear,
We have won the match, you got him out.
We'll get the trophy, how's that?

Joshua Walker (11)
Seabridge Primary School, Newcastle-under-Lyme

Feelings Inside So Strong

(Inspired by the song 'Something Inside So Strong' by Labi Siffre)

No matter what things I have to do;
The stronger I become,
Whatever the weather I'll succeed
My clouds will drift away,
No one can stop me
I keep going whatever comes my way -
You know, because there's . . .

Feelings inside so strong;
I know that I can do it.
Though, sometimes it's hard, so hard;
You thought that I'd just give up.
Oh no, feelings inside so strong
Oh, oh, oh, oh, oh, feelings inside so strong.

The more you push me to the limit;
I will keep fighting back,
Oh you hide yourself away from me
But I'm sure to find you,
You cannot hide away,
The rain keeps falling down,
My spark will shine so brightly
It will blind you,
'Cause there are . . .

Family and friends
They support me in everything I do;
I feel confident
Just have a go and say;
I'm gonna try it anyway.

Alana Walshaw (11)
Seabridge Primary School, Newcastle-under-Lyme

You're Looking Down On Me!

I found myself sat
In the front seat of the car
My dad took us to the park
And told us my nan has gone and died
All I know is I miss you so much
And I wish I could see you this once.

So I want you to know -
That I miss you so much
And that anywhere I am you will be
Always looking down on me!

You've seen my sister grow up
And I wish you could have seen me
Cos it's filled with funny moments here -
And odd sad moments there
But I believe that I will succeed!

So I want you to know -
That I miss you so much
And that anywhere I am you will be
Always looking down on me!

I'm really upset, that you have gone
But I'll believe in myself
And carry on.

So I want you to know
That I miss you so much
And that anywhere I am you will be
Always looking down on me!

Chelsey Tuff (11)
Seabridge Primary School, Newcastle-under-Lyme

Something Inside So Strong

(Inspired by the song 'Something Inside So Strong' by Labi Siffre)

My raindrops will get taken away -
By sun shining so bright.
I will try hard to concentrate -
To get a good level.
I will say I can.
I know you will do your best to help us.
No matter, cos there's . . .
All my friends that have been,
Through SATs said it's not that hard.
SATs is not as bad as options,
I hope I get a good score,
My family is there for me.
I shouldn't think it's going to be that hard.
I feel nervous when we do the test,
We have to do the test -
So we know our level for Year 7.
And good luck for the class!
Mr Robinson and
Mrs Watson will help you.
I will try hard.
Cos there's . . .

All my friends that have been
Through SATs said it's not that hard.
SATs is not as bad as options,
I hope I get a good score,
My family is there for me,
I shouldn't think it's going to be that hard.

Laura Field (11)
Seabridge Primary School, Newcastle-under-Lyme

Pets/Shoes - Haikus

Pets
Pets, pets, they're the best
Nice and cuddly, like to rest
They eat, sleep and drink.

Shoes
Lots of shoes to wear
I have at least 20 pairs
I love all my shoes.

Katrina Stokes (11)
Seabridge Primary School, Newcastle-under-Lyme

My Friends

Sitting with a friend, brilliant as a butterfly,
If I was a bird I would fly away to Hollywood,
The sparkling golden sunny Hollywood,
My friend is a frothy brown cappuccino,
If I argued with my friends,
I would swim the ocean twenty times to make up,
Friends are fab and brilliant,
Friends are crystal clear,
Friends are the best!

Alicia Hancock (9)
Seabridge Primary School, Newcastle-under-Lyme

Sport - Haikus

Sport is great, it rules,
Chelsea is my team they rule,
Get in there Chelsea.

I support Chelsea,
They are the champs, come on lads,
Come on Chelsea, yeah!

Kyle Clucas (11)
Seabridge Primary School, Newcastle-under-Lyme

Spiders

Spiders are my greatest fear,
When I look at one I'm screaming inside.
Their little tiny legs look like sharp nails,
Ready to rip me to shreds.

It makes me feel petrified thinking about them,
I imagine them as though they're as big as elephants,
With eight eyes and eight legs,
Not tiny like an ant.

It creeps closer to me,
Closer, closer, closer and,
Ouch! I scream as it bites me,
I run inside screaming, terrified and shocked.

The spiders win this time,
But next time I will squash them with my feet,
Spiders are my greatest fear,
Next time I won't be beat.

Hayley Shaw (10)
Seabridge Primary School, Newcastle-under-Lyme

Injections

Injections, injections are not my kind of thing,
I hate them in my leg,
I hate them in my arm.
I hate them so much
I really can't bear them.
They sting, they itch
They always hurt me.
Every time I sit in that chair
It always makes me nervous.
Injections, injections, are not my kind of thing.

Peter Wardle (10)
Seabridge Primary School, Newcastle-under-Lyme

Injections

Who would ever *want* an injection? I don't,
But if I want to go on holiday,
I have to have one today.

I walk into the doctors waiting room to see,
My mum's name appear onto the screen,
There it is on the screen,
My mum's name, I felt I could scream.

I walked down the passageway to door 4,
When I found it I tried to slip away on the floor,
But my mum grabbed me by the arm and thrust me past the door.

I walked into the room, my heart beating fast,
So I asked if I could go last.
'Okay I'll go first
But don't worry your arm won't burst.'

Then Mum's was over and done with,
My turn, now I'd love to be water and drain through a sieve,
I'm starting to shiver,
Like a leaf beginning to quiver.

It's coming towards me,
Sharp and pointy, shining in glee,
My tummy tightens in dread,
I'd rather be in bed.

It's enormous and awful,
Horrible and painful,
I feel upset
And then I start to fret.

The injection goes in,
My head starts to spin,
The injection comes out,
But I still have a doubt.

Gabrielle Andrews (10)
Seabridge Primary School, Newcastle-under-Lyme

Cats

Cats to me are great hairy beasts,
With claws that scratch, they're as sharp as needles,
And staring eyes.
If I see one on the street,
I shiver and get goosebumps on my arms.
My heart is pounding as I approach it,
My legs shake and shudder,
My knees turn to jelly,
I'm unable to walk.
My steps grow smaller, until they stop.
I haven't blinked for a minute.
I look around, heart pounding.
Where can I run? Backwards, forwards, up or down
I'm in a spin.
The cat walks past,
I close my eyes,
It purrs loudly.
I slowly open my eyes.
I turn around,
It's right behind me, ready to pounce!
I try too stay calm
But no, I can't!
I'm sweating, it's running down my cheeks,
Like a waterfall.
Then I scream . . . *Aaah!*
It gives one last purr
It felt like a day
It was only two minutes.
I think I've made it clear
Cats are my worst fear!

Sarah Peacock (9)
Seabridge Primary School, Newcastle-under-Lyme

China Dolls

I walk past a shop window,
There they sit . . . 30 of them!
Their beaming eyes staring at me,
I start to boil and shiver,
They start moving near me,
I start stamping my feet and jumping,
They start rolling their eyes,
I can feel my blood curdling,
I am trying to stop myself,
I started to panic,
Then all is quiet for a minute,
The china dolls *jump off the shelf!*
They start to walk towards me,
They break the window down,
And they come at me faster and faster,
At this moment I think I'm in a horror movie,
I can feel my hair standing on edge,
Then I know what they are,
They are china dolls.
Aaaaaagghhhhhh!

James Atkinson (10)
Seabridge Primary School, Newcastle-under-Lyme

Death

Death is a black shadow with a knife in its hand
Death is the scariest thing in all the land
I'm sitting in my bed awake
Wondering if the legends are fake
Then I hear a dreaded *bang!*
I see the unforgettable bloody fang
I look up and make a shriek!
And it looks like my veins are having a leak
It seems like Death has injected its venom
And then I simply go up to Heaven.

Aiden Bennett (10)
Seabridge Primary School, Newcastle-under-Lyme

Wasps

My greatest fear is wasps,
I hate their dreadful stings,
They buzz around my head,
They are such horrid things.

When they are coming at me,
I make myself stand still,
I really feel uncomfortable,
They make me feel quite ill.

When I have a picnic,
They land upon my food,
They dance on it with dirty feet,
And I think that that's quite rude.

They make me feel terrified,
Scared out of my wits,
Screaming, hiding, petrified,
This really is the pits.

Their black and yellow uniform,
Is a warning to us all,
Just roll up that old newspaper,
And *splat* them on the wall!

Megan Allingham (10)
Seabridge Primary School, Newcastle-under-Lyme

My Friend

My friend makes me feel as happy as a monkey swinging
In a joyful, jangling jungle.
If I ever fell out with my friend, I would climb Mount Everest.

My friend makes me feel as cheerful as a kangaroo jumping.
My friend is a joyful, jumping jaguar.
My friend likes being a monkey called Elvis.

My friend's name is . . .
Liam!

Jason Hamer (9)
Seabridge Primary School, Newcastle-under-Lyme

Friends

Friends are people who look out for you,
Friends play with you
They always stick up for you.

That's friends for you!

Friends tell the truth when it's bad,
Friends share secrets and never tell
You can see through friends, crystal clear
Friends cheer you up when you're down.

That's friends for you!

Friends have things in common
Friends call for you
Friends never give up on you.

That's friends for you!

Jake Taylor (9)
Seabridge Primary School, Newcastle-under-Lyme

Ventriloquist Dummies

Ventriloquist dummies are freaky and weird
They freak me out,
I despise them so much that I run at the first chance.
I really do detest ventriloquist dummies.
I so loathe ventriloquist dummies
The way they creek their necks
And look at you with their big bold eyes.
They make me sweat and my mouth feels dry and sickly.
I grab the first thing to hand and swing, swing, and swing just in case.
Their eyes look at me and I sense something behind me.
So I run, run and run and don't look back at all.

Jacob Hampton (10)
Seabridge Primary School, Newcastle-under-Lyme

Spiders

Spiders are black and blood-curdling beasts
That make my hairs prickle on the back of my neck.
As gruesome as they are crawling in my room
Making me scream.
Spiders, spiders, all around me
Spiders, spiders.

Black widows,
Big ones,
Small ones,
Fat ones,
Thin ones,
Scary ones,
Hairy ones,
And that makes me feel sick
And that's spiders
The blood-curdling beast.

Jessica Heath (10)
Seabridge Primary School, Newcastle-under-Lyme

Injections

Oh no, it's injection day,
I don't want to have one.
I hate their pointed ends
And their grey and silver colour.
Doctors, nurses and anyone else.
I hate them all.

They hurt your arm, when they go in like a dagger.
As the needle goes in out comes a massive
'Argh!'
The pain is over in seconds,
But not for me because as you know
I really hate injections.

Emma Hunt (10)
Seabridge Primary School, Newcastle-under-Lyme

The Friendless Girl

I'm the friendless girl,
I have no friends you see,
The problem is I'm really shy,
I just can't chat, chat, chat.

But that was then
And now is now . . .

I have been in this class for quite a few years,
But I still have no friends at all,
All of break I sit on a bench all alone,
It's all coming back to me now.

But that was then
And now is now . . .

I live a lonely lifestyle,
My parents have died too,
And I live in a care home,
With nobody my age or size.

But that was then,
And now is now . . .

I was a lonely sheep,
Lost from the flock,
Until she came
A girl, my age and size.

But that was then,
And now is now . . .

I've got a friend,
Sally is her name,
We like the same things,
And are in the same class!

But that was then,
And now is now . . .

Sally is Miss Popular,
She's helped me make friends,
She's good at everything,
Plus really kind and helpful.

But that was then,
And now is now . . .

I've got no room mate anymore,
Sally's been adopted,
But I'm really glad she came,
Because I'm not the friendless girl anymore!

I'm as happy as a bee,
But I miss Sally lots,
So it cheered me up to find,
Sally is my *penfriend!*

Rachel Eatough (10)
Seabridge Primary School, Newcastle-under-Lyme

My Friend

My friend is fun,
She is cool,
If I never had a friend
I'd be a fool.

My friend is kind,
A delicious cocktail,
If there was a friend contest
We'd never fail.

My friend is cheerful,
As joyful as a smile,
When we fall out and make up
I say 'I'm that sorry I'd swim the River Nile.'

My friend is smart,
We love to dance,
We go to ballet,
I do a perfect point then prance.

This poem,
Is about my friend and me
It is a brilliant poem
As you can see!

Hannah Wain (10)
Seabridge Primary School, Newcastle-under-Lyme

Mum

I always felt secure as a brick wall when you are around me.
I am the calm sea, lapping against the sand.
When you're not around, no one could replace you in my heart.

When you're around me, I feel invincible.
When you're not around, I am afraid.
When you're around me, I feel safe.
When you're around me, you make me laugh.

When you're around me, you make me as happy as a dolphin.
When you're not around me, I feel lonely.
When you're around me, I feel full.

When you're around, I feel fine.
When you're around me, I feel like having the time of my life.
When you're around me, I feel complete.
It's crystal-clear, that you are here, thanks.

Joseph Harris (10)
Seabridge Primary School, Newcastle-under-Lyme

Injections, Horrid Injections

Injections would make me breathless,
My heart would beat like a drum,
I'd hear the headaching sound of an alarm
Closer and closer I'm getting more stressful,
I just want to run and never come back.

Why a needle? Can't it be something less painful?
I'd yell, I'd scream, I'd fall to the ground.
I'm petrified the needle has gone in, I'm in pain,
I can't even move, my spine is tingling,
My blood is curdling, my heart is stopping.

I feel doomed, I'm making strange reactions,
But I know it's all over but I hope it never happens again.
I am less petrified, my heart starts again
My spine stops to tingle and I'm all calm now.

Aaron Jones (10)
Seabridge Primary School, Newcastle-under-Lyme

Injections

My fear is injections
They are not my thing
Every time I go into the waiting room
I feel like I'm going to scream!
My mum says I'll be OK
It's not the end of the world
But I think it is.

I'm still in the waiting room
It has been five minutes
Then I hear my name being called
So I slowly stand up
And step by step I slowly walk
Forward
My heart starts to beat like a drum.

The nurse says, 'Hello, how do you do?'
I want to reply, 'Horrid thank you.'
I sit on a chair, in a small room
She gets the biggest needle *ever!*
It slowly comes closer and closer
Until I let out a scream
But then I realise it hasn't began
I close my eyes and the needle
Prickles the top of my skin
It feels like a hedgehog
I scream, it's finally over.

Jessica Hollingworth (10)
Seabridge Primary School, Newcastle-under-Lyme

Fear!

Fear is black.
It tastes like an uncooked burger
And it smells like rotten skin.
Fear looks like a rotten goblin.
It sounds like a werewolf howling.
It feels like an iron sword.

Nathan James (9)
Seabridge Primary School, Newcastle-under-Lyme

Run! Monsters!

'Oh, I'm bored, I want to read my book,'
I said at 10 o'clock last night.
'The only thing is, is that my book is upstairs
And up there, there is no light.'
So I sat,
But soon,
I got rather sleepy,
So I decided to face the stairs and *by gum!* they were creepy.
A while later, I reached my room and I opened the door so slight,
Grabbed my book, looked at it, then gave a shriek of fright!
You are doomed!
We are the monsters!
Said the cover that was written in blood,
I gasped!
I dropped the book and then . . .
Ran!
I ran out of my room, down the stairs
And made an awful din.
I went into the lounge, locked the door,
But then . . . *boom!*
The monsters came running in!

Alex Lister (10)
Seabridge Primary School, Newcastle-under-Lyme

Injections

Injections, injections I really hate
They make you sit in the room and wait
The pointed sharp end of the needle gives me the shivers
As it begins to move very, very slowly to my arm,
My blood goes cold as ice, my hair sticks just like
I've been struck by lightning and my heart thumps like a drum.
As the needle gets closer and closer I close my eyes
And when the needle strikes into me I let out a big yell!
And when the needle comes out I can't stop shivering
That's why I dread injections.

Ciaran Edwards (10)
Seabridge Primary School, Newcastle-under-Lyme

Always Work Hard

The harder and better you practise -
The better you become.
At Shugbrough, have confidence at all times,
Do your best, never stop.
You can have my rights,
In SATs concentrate and keep your head up.
Always believe . . .

At all times work hard -
Keep climbing up the mountain,
If you keep believing in hard work,
You will get a good SATs mark.
Oh no, all work is so strong,
Oh, oh, oh, keep working at all times.

Higher the mountain you have to climb -
The harder it will be.
Keep climbing all the way, don't stop.
Don't give up or keep tumbling,
Keep going to the top.
You can always do it,
I will always try the best I can -
And never stop
And always believe it.

Jack Burton (11)
Seabridge Primary School, Newcastle-under-Lyme

Siblings

S melly, stinky, sweaty and stupid
I diotic, interfering
B ossy, boring beasts
L ooney, lazy losers
I nconsiderate and thoughtless
N osy, noisy and very naughty
G ross, gibbering, greedy gorillas
S ometimes I wish I'm an only child.

Imaan Ahmad
Seabridge Primary School, Newcastle-under-Lyme

Spiders

Spiders!
Hairy, crawling monsters
As evil as the *Devil*
Life-destroying creatures
I *hate* them
Spiders!
Black, ugly things
The colour of death
As quick as the *flash!*
I *hate* them . . .
Spiders!
If I see a spider
Voom!
I'm gone!
I hate spiders!

Joshua Bailey (9)
Seabridge Primary School, Newcastle-under-Lyme

Hospitals

Hospitals! Hospitals!
They smell horrible;
They makes me feel sick inside
Hospitals! Hospitals!
They give you injections
They really do hurt
Hospitals! Hospitals!
They make my mouth water
And taste like a slug
I walk in the room
It's as spooky as Hell
I could die!
Nee-naw, nee-naw, nee-naw.

Courtney Harvey (10)
Seabridge Primary School, Newcastle-under-Lyme

My Fear Of Injections

I hate injections.
They make me tremble and scared,
I'd never ever have one,
Even if I was *dared!*

Injections are heart stopping,
Petrifying and frightening.
When the needle sticks in me,
I always shout, '*Ahhhhh*.'

There, there it's all over,
No more anxious moments.

Doctors, dentists, nurses.
They are all ready to pounce.
Needles at the ready,
Mum says, 'Just keep still.'

When the needle is out,
I feel shocked and light-headed,
I get off the bed,
Struggling to walk.

Chris Durose (10)
Seabridge Primary School, Newcastle-under-Lyme

Heights!

Heights! Heights! are *not* cool,
Heights! Heights! I'd rather go to school,
Don't put me on the Eiffel Tower, that's a fact,
'Cause I'll react!
If I was told to step out and jump,
Whoever told me they'd won themselves a big
. . . *thump!*

Heights! Heights! are as big as a giraffe
Heights! Heights! make me tremble like jelly
I'd rather stay at home and watch telly
Heights! Heights! are not cool.

Amy Spencer (9)
Seabridge Primary School, Newcastle-under-Lyme

Friends

Friends are good,
Friends are cool,
Have fun with friends,
They aren't cruel.

But friends, when they're feeling down,
You don't know why and you will frown.

Some friends are happy, some are sad,
They sometimes argue, that's not good,
But they're still the happiest friends I have,
I can't imagine life without friends.

But friends when they're feeling bad,
It takes away every good time you had.

Friends are nice, who I like,
They are curious cats,
Who love to have fun.

But friends when they're feeling down,
You don't know why and you will frown.

Laura Shallcross (9)
Seabridge Primary School, Newcastle-under-Lyme

Don't Know What Is Behind You

Have you ever had that feeling there's something behind you? I have.
I was all alone in the evening,
Then the lights switched off.
I went out and switched them on.
My stomach started to turn, so I walked over to the door
And I couldn't open it.

My dad came back and the door finally opened.
It came to my bedtime so I went to switch my light off.
My spine went cold; my stomach felt like someone was
squeezing it tight.
Finally I had the courage to switch off the light.
But that night I just couldn't sleep.

Thomas Durham (10)
Seabridge Primary School, Newcastle-under-Lyme

Hairy Little Pests

Hairy little pests at the end of my bed
Further they get
I'm cold and shivery
They're glad we met.
Moving slowly I get back
Further they get.

I get up and jump and hide.
I hear large legs hitting the floor.
Swinging in his web, it swings around the corner,
Scowls at me.
His big sharp claws digging in the ground.
I'm sitting holding my knees, I'm sweating, shivering,
What is it going to do next?
My heart is pumping
His eight eyes glancing up and down
Ready to pounce on me.
I jumped over the settee
He runs around the settee.
I run upstairs, hide in my cupboard
I hear *tap, tap, tap* on the cupboard door
I swung the door and nothing was there!

Ethan Joseph (9)
Seabridge Primary School, Newcastle-under-Lyme

Mosquitoes

Mosquitoes come out at night, crawl up your back and give you a fright.

They're itchy, hairy and vicious too.
They suck your blood, that's not very nice for you.
They're big and hard and smell like lard.
They're bumpy and spiky and give you lumps.
You can feel them, they're like bumps
So remember if you ever see one, just . . .
Run!

Layla Ayub (9)
Seabridge Primary School, Newcastle-under-Lyme

The Dark

The dark, the dark is not my thing,
My heart beats like an African drum
Getting faster and faster . . . until boom!
What's that?
I stop, dead as dead as a feather in the mud . . .
Boom!
There it goes again, I take one small step.
At this moment my hands are sweating,
I squeeze my teddy so very hard.
The dark, the dark is definitely not my thing,
I feel like running away, to hide from whatever is . . .
But what is there?
I reach for a light switch . . . but no, there's not one there,
I'm trembling with fear.
I daren't run, a cold breeze brushes over me.
I put my nails into my mouth, I bite until there's nothing left.
The dark is definitely, definitely not my thing.
'There's nothing there, there's nothing there,' I whisper under my breath.
My ears are more sensitive than they have ever been in my life,
In fact all my senses are picking anything up.
My eyes stay wide as a big ripe apple.
I'm getting goosebumps, I can feel them getting bigger and bigger.
I feel like I'm in the middle of the woods at the dead of night.
The dark, the dark is definitely, definitely, definitely not my thng.

Edward Jones (10)
Seabridge Primary School, Newcastle-under-Lyme

Haikus

Football is the best
Chelsea is my favourite
Come on the Chelsea!

I love gymnastics
Gymnastics is really fun
I will try my best!

Louis Downs (11)
Seabridge Primary School, Newcastle-under-Lyme

Heights

Up and up I go higher and higher
I'm at the top, oh dear
I feel quite queer.

I'm with my mate Mick,
I feel quite sick,
I'm standing on a glass floor,
Great there's the door.

I say, 'Can I come down?'
'No way,' said my mum
I feel quite dumb.

Oh no, what's that trickling
Down my leg?
It's wet and it smells a lot,
I feel like a little tot.

Then it gets worse
The wind is picking up
All I can hear is my heart beating
And sweat pouring off my head.

Then I shout,
'Get me down from here!'

Bradley Godbold (10)
Seabridge Primary School, Newcastle-under-Lyme

Snakes

Snakes are my worst fear,
It's gliding towards me and I'm getting scared,
I can feel my heart thumping and I find that I am biting my nails,
Its body is rough and scaly,
Its eyes are green and evil,
And it is suddenly coming closer and closer, and it wraps round my legs.

It hisses and I run away
Snakes are definitely my worst fear.

Emma Shallcross (9)
Seabridge Primary School, Newcastle-under-Lyme

Who Is My Friend?

My friend to me is as cheerful as a smiling clown,
Always makes me laugh.
I would like to go to wet, windy Wales with my friend,
So we could have a fun time together,
Like two busy bees making honey.

I like to play football with my friend especially when we
Score goals against each other.
We have arguments, like a raging ocean,
Trying to drown people ashore.
He is a soothing hot chocolate that understands me.
I would be there for my friend, if they lost someone close to them
Or they were sad.

Adam Shann (9)
Seabridge Primary School, Newcastle-under-Lyme

Good Friends

He puts a happy smile on my face
He'll win any race
He likes to go to the cinema
He will sit there eating a chocolate bar
He likes to be a chef, or a cook,
He gets lots of luck!
He has long blond hair
He will scream at a ride at the fair
He does not like school
But he is very cool
Me and him are gonna make a den
That's why his name is Ben.

Alex Clewlow
Seabridge Primary School, Newcastle-under-Lyme

My Mystery Friend

My mystery friend has short brown hair,
She's so cheeky, she'll do any dare,
She's as funny as a teacher doing the chicken dance.

My mystery friend's name starts with 'Je' and ends with 'ss'
She's as cool as ice,
And she's as fit as a fiddle.

My mystery friend is as quiet as a mouse,
She's like Blackpool as bright as a light,
And she's as tall as the Eiffel Tower
        And that's my mystery friend.

Emily Taylor (10)
Seabridge Primary School, Newcastle-under-Lyme

Snakes

Snakes! Snakes! Slithery snakes are not so cool
I rather go to gymnastics school.
Fangs them big things fangs!
Sharp poisonous oh no.
I don't like snakes, they're horrible, horrible.
I do not like snakes!
Goosebumps on my arms, butterflies in my tum.
Snakes! Snakes! Snakes! Snakes!

Chloe Entwistle (10)
Seabridge Primary School, Newcastle-under-Lyme

Sport - Haiku

Sport is very good;
Football, cricket and rugby -
Very good indeed!

Daniel King (11)
Seabridge Primary School, Newcastle-under-Lyme

My Best Friends

My best friend makes me as happy as a clown,
The happiest clown in the whole world,
When you are around me I feel as safe as a star in the enormous sky.

If I could run with my friends,
As fast as a cheetah,
I would run to beautiful bluey *Blackpool.*

I would like to teach my friends boxing,
They make me feel like the truest friend on Earth.

When they have lost somebody,
I would stick by them like nothing has ever happened
And every single one of my friends are cool.

Daniel Burton (10)
Seabridge Primary School, Newcastle-under-Lyme

The Lost Soul

It is as dark as the night sky,
The taste is a sour lemon,
It is as dark as the Devil's heart,
The smell is as bad as a dead fox lying in the sun,
The feeling is worse than brains in a blender,
It sounds worse then a screeching cat at dawn,
It reminds me of zombies shouting in the claws of Hell.

It feels as bad as the Devil's heartbeat,
The smell is of blood, rotten blood,
It looks worse than brains scattered on the floor,
The taste is worse than the Devil in the pit of Hell,
The sound is as bad as a cat in the claws of Hell.

Liam Potts (11)
Two Gates Community Primary School, Tamworth

Darkness

Darkness is a pool of ink.
It tastes like water drooling from a sink.
It looks of people shrinking really small.
It smells of my mum's pie which really drives me up the wall.
It feels of sweat dripping off my face
It sounds of music at a really slow pace.
It reminds me of the time I fell down a black hole
And sucking out my little living soul.

Laura Donnelly (11)
Two Gates Community Primary School, Tamworth

Fun

Fun feels like butterflies in your stomach,
It smells of sparklers just gone off,
It looks as if fireworks are flying through the air,
Tastes of fizzy pop bubbling in your mouth,
It sounds like laughter in the background,
It reminds me of when I went to Alton Towers.

Josh Thomson (11)
Two Gates Community Primary School, Tamworth

Fun

It tastes of freedom
It looks really cool
It smells of fresh air
It feels like a hug from Mum
It sounds of people laughing
It reminds me of a cheeseburger treat.

Bradley Weddell (10)
Two Gates Community Primary School, Tamworth

Gloom And Doom

Fear is black, a black hole in a tornado.
It feels like you're standing alone, in a haunted forest.
It smells of the sweat dripping off your face.
It looks as though you can see a faint shadow of . . . *a ghost!*
The door creaked and slammed shut!
It tastes of the cold, bitter air brushing past your mouth,
Gasping as it takes your breath away.
It sounds of the breezy wind,
Whistling through the twisted branches of a thousand-year-old tree.
It reminds me of the time my sister told me a story, I never forgot.

Hate is black and blue, a bruised eye.
It feels as if it's trapping you and your enemy
In a gloomy minute closet.
It looks as though it's going to hit you back in the face,
A fist ready to punch.
It tastes of sweet revenge and hatred in your eyes.
It smells of the food you most hate,
The cabbage you feed your dog under the table.
It sounds of the voice,
The slow and croaky voice of your worst enemy.
It reminds me of the feeling, the feeling inside,
The feeling is hate, anything but pride.

Bethany Taylor (11)
Two Gates Community Primary School, Tamworth

Fun

Is the colour of the sun
It feels like a great big smile
It smells of a great big McDonald's
It looks like two arms coming to tickle me
It tastes of smooth soft milkshake
It sounds of a plucked guitar
It reminds me of a birthday party

Luke Johnson (11)
Two Gates Community Primary School, Tamworth

Emotions

Fear
Fear is black, dark as a night's sky,
It tastes of an emotion, an emotion that's not high.
Fear looks unhappy, something that's wrong,
It smells of unwelcoming, of something that's too strong.
Fear itself feels scared, it doesn't know what's right,
It reminds me of death, wondering what happens next.

Love
Love is a rainbow, a rainbow high in the sky,
It smells of confetti, confetti that's so bright.
Love looks so airy, a smile that never dies,
It tastes of sweet roses, a taste that cannot lie.
Love sounds so joyful, joyful, jolly and great,
It reminds me of my family, and my family can never break.

Sadness
Sadness is a blue, a blue that's so cold,
It smells of unhappiness, that's not been told.
Sadness looks so heartbroken, and destroyed,
It tastes of sheer bitterness, bitterness and annoyed.
Sadness sounds so quiet, so quiet and alone,
It reminds me of being alone, all on my own.

Neena Johal (11)
Two Gates Community Primary School, Tamworth

Darkness

Darkness is black as a black hole
It smells like a smoking skull
It looks like nothing as I am suffering
It tastes as bad as slimy goo
It sounds like devils are calling
It feels as squidgy as the Devil's heart.

Jake Wright (10)
Two Gates Community Primary School, Tamworth

Darkness Is Anger

Darkness is pitch-black
It looks deadly dynamite about to explode!
It sounds terrifying the black hole is calling *me!*
It smells like dark black smoke!
It feels as if someone is tapping *me!*
It tastes of something gone off!
It reminds me of when I trapped my finger in my car door!

Anger is red, red as blood!
It feels bubbly, and squidgy like glue!
It sounds like a whisper going down my neck!
It smells of something burning maybe tyres!
It tastes of a manky bowl of soup!
It reminds me of when I got hit by a car!

Luke Wright (10)
Two Gates Community Primary School, Tamworth

Darkness

Hate
Hate is dark black and gloomy,
It tastes so bad you can't eat it
It looks so bad worse than an alien on a good day
It smells as bad as a storage station
It feels like a horrible death
It sounds like a horrible scream
It reminds me of a big fight

Anger
Anger is dark as a black hole full of enemies
It tastes so hot it will make you breathe fire
It looks as if you entered a world without beauty
It smells so bad it's like the air is polluted
It feels like a mouldy biscuit, getting squashed when I stand on it
It sounds like someone dying,
It reminds me of a funeral.

Ashley Beale (10)
Two Gates Community Primary School, Tamworth

Love

Love is yellow and mellow, makes you red on your face,
It tastes so sweet like a sugar beet,
It looks at you as the romance flows through,
It smells of perfume from your girl in full bloom,
It feels all funny like a tickle in your tummy,
It sounds so cool as you both jump in the pool,
And sweet love reminds you of the best time of your life
. . . *Love!*

Benjamin Swaby (11)
Two Gates Community Primary School, Tamworth

Love Reminds Me?

Love sounds as if a little person jumps and grabs your heart,
Love feels as if you will never be alone - by yourself,
Love smells sweeter than chocolate, melting in your mouth,
Love looks at you while you do your hair, as you look in the mirror,
Love tastes as I eat some Turkish Delight, but I like it when it is true,
Love's colour is a ravishing-red just like a heart,
Love reminds me of a beautiful heart going into the proper shape of
Valentines.

Aimee Shortman (11)
Two Gates Community Primary School, Tamworth

Hunger

Hunger is chewy brown, it oozes through your glittery teeth,
It feels of a screaming bat, biting you in the heart,
It smells of a tramp, drinking fluids,
It looks of a juicy double burger, dribbling from your mouth,
It tastes of a lemon, shaking your head side to side with its sour,
It sounds like a ghost playing jittery old organs,
It reminds me of a nerve racking suspicious movie I watched.

Daniel Davis (11)
Two Gates Community Primary School, Tamworth

Fun

Fun is the colour of the sun bright and extremely hot.
Fun tastes as if we were eating lovely creamy chocolate.
Fun looks like people picking little flowers, making pretty
Daisy chains.
Fun smells as if I am helping my mum to make
A cooked dinner.
It reminds me of my dog and playing fetch with him.
Feels like I am jumping in a swimming pool, and everyone who's
Dry getting them wet.
Fun sounds as if people are really happy and jolly.

Catherine Brown (11)
Two Gates Community Primary School, Tamworth

Dark Black

Darkness is dark as a pitch-black hole
It looks like a black hole
It smells of burning wood
It looks like a giant black figure standing there
It tastes like pieces of things burning
It sounds like a big creepy man
It reminds me of the air raid.

Nathan Gilliver (11)
Two Gates Community Primary School, Tamworth

Silence

Its silence white as white can be . . . !
It sounds so quiet, quiet as can be . . . !
It feels so emotional, emotional like me . . . !
It looks so blank, blank as can be . . . !
It tastes so empty, empty as can be . . . !
It smells so boring, boring as she . . . !
It reminds me of tasteless food for my tea . . . !

Cally Lockington (10)
Two Gates Community Primary School, Tamworth

The Dark Hole Anger

It tastes the same as vomit,
It looks the same as an atomic bomb about to blow,
It feels as if it was a brain squirting blood out of it,
It sounds like a pig being stabbed in the heart,
It smells as if it was the pit of Hell,
It reminds me of my mum's cooking.

Connor Willson (11)
Two Gates Community Primary School, Tamworth

Fear

Fear is black, full of loneliness,
It smells vile just like a pile of dirty old socks,
It looks like a set of eyes faced on you,
It tastes as if blood is dripping from your own mouth,
It feels as if someone is squeezing you as hard as they possibly can,
It sounds of a strange voice whispering my name,
It reminds me of being all by myself scared, is something in here with me?

Zoe Priseman (10)
Two Gates Community Primary School, Tamworth

Love

Love is a deep red, a passionate emotion,
It tastes, a fun sweet chocolate when you want to have more,
It looks warm, a duvet made of roses without thorns,
It smells delightful when you take a whiff, you feel weak but gentle,
It feels romantic, feel love and you feel you're on top of the world,
It sounds like birds chirping, as if their worries have flown away,
It reminds me of a roller coaster, you don't know what to expect,
Will be fun or dangerous?

Alison Jennings (11)
Two Gates Community Primary School, Tamworth

Laughter

Laughter is the yellow of a smiley face, jumping with joy
It looks like the Joker and his devilish laugh
It feels as if someone is tickling you over and over again
and you're trying to stop them
It tastes like eating laughter gum, and trying to spit it out
It sounds like one million people laughing at the same joke, with
funny tones
It smells as if there is a lovely cake, ready to burst into laughter
It reminds me of the time I was laughing for half an hour.

Jack Hudson (10)
Two Gates Community Primary School, Tamworth

Mallard

M allard moves out of London
A ttracting people to take pictures
L ondon to Edinburgh it's non-stop-run
L uxury for the passengers in the dining car
A rriving in style with crowds cheering
R ecord broken from London to Edinburgh
D ry in the National Railway Museum safe from scrap.

Timmy Taylor (8)
Wigmore Primary School, Leominster

Cricket

C urling the ball on the wicket
R unning for the stump
I s it out? Who knows
C rikey nearly lbw
K ick the ball, ow!
E arly afternoon, time for lunch
T eatime nearly here, yippee
Oh we're 500 runs behind.

Russell Woolley (8)
Wigmore Primary School, Leominster

My Dump Of A Bedroom

I slowly open the white painted door and tiptoe into the room,
Scattered sulvaineoins spike my feet,
Quickly get out the brisk broom.
Spindly spiders scuttle secretly,
Beach balls bounce and boom.

I walk further into doom.
My bedroom swallows me up,
Drifting dust covers my keyboard with a blanket of grey,
The cat's fluffy fur, covers my gorgeous bed.
Cracked crazy colourful cups sit on the towering shelves.
Bullying, bulky boots fight over space.

I look loopy while I hide under my bed
From an army of teddies,
Sleeping,
Creeping,
Watching spying on my every step,
Just watching me and my kitten.

Jasmine Hodges (10)
Wigmore Primary School, Leominster

Rambler

R aging old train
A s strong as an oak
M ountain climber
B ellowing pistons
L oading the goods
E ngine hissing
R ambler.

William Dartnell (8)
Wigmore Primary School, Leominster

Dinky

Sleepy, cheeky
Chewing, jumping, playing
I watch her run and chase her tail
That's her.

Nicola Lawther (8)
Wigmore Primary School, Leominster

Donkey

Floppy ears,
Leaping, kicking, jumping
Swishing his tail from the flies
Eyore!

Ebony Brown (9)
Wigmore Primary School, Leominster

Sheepy

Woolly and white
Grazing, dreaming, running
I hope they will help me sleep tight,
Baa! Baa!

Ross Hurley (8)
Wigmore Primary School, Leominster

Puppy

Cute, small, fluffy,
Ball of fur waddling,
Tail constantly waggling,
Sniff, sniff.

Natalie Jones (9)
Wigmore Primary School, Leominster

Pony

Fierce, cheeky,
Kicking, neighing, swishing
Galloping in the bright sunshine,
Neigh! Neigh!

Kitty Phillips (8)
Wigmore Primary School, Leominster

Giraffe

Tall, patterned,
Bending, trotting, snatching
Leaves from the Acacia tree.
Stretch.

Lucy Knight-Summers (8)
Wigmore Primary School, Leominster

Puppy

Cold and wet nose,
My cute licking machine,
I play with him after school,
Woof! Woof!

Natasha Thomas (9)
Wigmore Primary School, Leominster

Tiger

Stripy, prowler,
Bounding, roaring, leaping,
Skulking through the deep rainforest,
Pounce!

Joseph Bicknell (8)
Wigmore Primary School, Leominster

ABC Poem

A is for Adam the ant who is busy
B is for Ben the bear who is dizzy
C is for Caroline the cat who is snoozing
D is for Daniel the dog who's been boozing
E is for Edward the elephant so tall
F is for Freddy the frog who's so small
G is for Gordon the guinea pig so fat
H is for Harriet the hedgehog who's sat
I is for Iris the iguana in the sun
J is for James the jackdaw having fun
K is for Kate the kiwi who's rustling
L is for Lucy the lemur who's bustling
M is for Megan the monkey who's swinging
N is for Natasha the newt who's grinning
O is for Olwen the otter who's swimming
P is for Peter the poodle who's trimming
Q is for Queeny the quail who is pecking
R is for Ross the rabbit who's wrecking
S is for Sam the snake who is slithering
T is for Tim the tarantula who is dithering
U is for Ursula the unicorn who's flying
V is for Victoria the vallhund who's buying
W is for Will the whelk who's stuck
X is for Xander who's really a duck
Y is for Yella a yak who is grumpy
Z is for Zara the zebra who's jumpy.

Holly Watkins (9)
Wigmore Primary School, Leominster

Zebra

Busy stripes
Trotting, swishing, running
Across the plains of Africa
Wild!

Enola Wallis (8)
Wigmore Primary School, Leominster

My Bedroom

I stand in my bedroom,
Looking at the floor,
It is very, very messy,
From the window to the door.

Muddy paw prints over bed covers,
From where the cat has been,
Toy mice all over the carpet,
It is a messy scene.

My teddy bears abandoned on the floor,
They lie there day and night,
Collecting dust,
It isn't a pretty sight.

Glasses and glasses of lemonade,
Perched up on the window sill,
Probably out of date,
But in one lives my fish Gill.

A mountain of socks piled up high,
They smell like a skunk,
My mum washes them,
But now they have shrunk!

So that's my bedroom,
Smelly and stinky isn't it?
But I like it even though . . .
It's a tip!

Chloe Matthews (10)
Wigmore Primary School, Leominster

Spiders

Tiny, spooky
Creeping, crawling, sneaking,
Why do they live under my bed?
Silent.

Connie Alder (8)
Wigmore Primary School, Leominster

My Brother's Bedroom

A stinking whiff of slimy, smelly socks,
Magazines half read blocking the bed and the luxury light,
The telly and the Xbox crushed in the corner
Clothes crying out in the drawers wanting to be worn.

An army of broken toys marching to the bin,
Just another one to be lost and put back in,
Old clothes hiding the well worn floor,
The creaking of the floorboards above the kitchen door,
Wardrobes whipping open and closed,
Monopoly money whining to be put back in the box.

Olivia Edwards (9)
Wigmore Primary School, Leominster

My Bedroom

The smell of dust in the air,
The sound of a bat above my head in the middle of the night,
Sounds banging like a dinosaur in the middle of the night,
The squeak, squeak of the guinea pigs
Just outside my bedroom window,
Socks that smell like cheese squashed into the carpet,
Toilet roll in bits crunched up in balls like sleeping hedgehogs.

Caleb Roberts (9)
Wigmore Primary School, Leominster

Horses

H ooves clicking on the tarmac lane
O ver and under plaiting the mane
R eins pulling hard and tight
S addles, shining, polished bright
E ating, chewing all day long
S tables smelly, what a pong!

Rosie Trounson (8)
Wigmore Primary School, Leominster

My Bedroom

When I stroll through my bedroom door I see . . .
My messy bed,
Unmade,
The duvet half on, half off.

Cat paw prints everywhere,
Toast stuck to the carpet almost if it's glued there.

My CD player making a whirring noise,
Socks scattered under my bed.

My football boots all muddy,
Rotting away in the corner,
My clock *tick-tock, tick-tock* all day and night.

Pictures hanging from one corner.

Hannah Segar (9)
Wigmore Primary School, Leominster

Rabbits

Rabbits in the wild
Rabbits running free
Hiding in their warren
Deep beneath a tree.

Rabbits having lunch
Rabbits having dinner
Rabbits having races
And being the winner.

So now I would like a rabbit of my own
I could see it every day
I'd feed it and play with it
Any colour, white, black or grey.

Starting today!

Delya Joubert (9)
Wigmore Primary School, Leominster

My Bedroom

When I look into my room I see . . .
Smelly socks, a mouldy banana skin,
A dusty TV, muddy paw prints,
Stinky smelly perfume,
A coffee-stained T-shirt,
A muddy slimy football
Rolling across the floor,
Smelly red wellies,
Toffee sweets squashed into the
Creamy-coloured carpet,
A parade of toys,
Dog hairs on the carpet,
Ripped pages from a book,
Rubbish scattered all over the floor,
Grubby computer, dusty make-up,
Fluffy cats scratching my lovely bed,
Lemonade drink from an empty cup,
Ripped posters scattered
All over the floor,
Ripped pillow cases,
Feathers dropping like sparkles of snow.

Gabrielle Hince (10)
Wigmore Primary School, Leominster

Glue

There was a young boy, little Lou
Who slipped in a pot of glue
His feet were so sticky
He found it quite tricky
To put his feet back in his shoe.

Louis Williams (8)
Wigmore Primary School, Leominster

What Am I?

Button . . . pressed *on!*
Humming to begin with,
Buzzing then roaring!
Chasing, chasing its prey,
Then, lashing out viciously, pouncing!
Gulps, then swallows,
Killer of dust and dirt, mud and fluff.
Then belching, burping,
Coughing, sneezing, spluttering,
A tickle in its throat.
Then . . .
What's that stench?
Tracking it down,
Its long silver and black head,
Slithering along,
The innocent operator trailing helplessly behind,
For the monster has a mind of its own!
Found it!
A long-lost sock, *yum!*
Sucking it in, drawing in breath . . .
Stuck.
Eyes watering, who cares?
Tired now, tired as rust,
Out come the leads -
From the silently greedy plug holes.
Coming to a halt
Sleep at last!

Laura Johnson (11)
Wigmore Primary School, Leominster

William

My best friend Will
Trainspotter, spotting trains
A super mad top cyclist too!
Choo! Choo!

Sam Davies (8)
Wigmore Primary School, Leominster

My Bedroom

I stand at my door,
Looking down at the purple floor,
Teddies fill my room like a class of school children,
A TV covered in a blanket of glistening dust . . .
My bin explodes with litter like a volcano,
A whining wardrobe swallows my clothes,
Books piled high, transformed into Mount Everest,
Sweaty socks lying exhausted in a heap,
Apple cores in my drawers,
Creased clean clothes lying abandoned,
Schoolwork that hasn't made its way to my desk,
Rusty, dusty radio lies on my floor,
Empty cardboard boxes running across my carpet,
Chocolate squelched into the rug,
My bed covers block the door,
Windows are surrounded by pens.
Pets scattered across the floor.

Abbigail Beamond (9)
Wigmore Primary School, Leominster

The Peregrine Falcon

P erching on the old wooden post
E agerly searching for its prey
R acing, stooping - 100 miles an hour
E ventually levelling out
G rasping the pigeon in its talons
R ipping its prey with its hooked beak
I n its nest safe with its chick on the tip of the cliff
N ever losing control - beady-eyed
E nthusiastic hunter of the sky.

Edward Humphreys (9)
Wigmore Primary School, Leominster

My Bedroom

I stand at my blue bedroom door,
Looking down at the floor . . .

A flowery fragrance, floating round the room,
A clock with no batteries lying in a corner of gloom,
Lovely, lilac lipstick, lounging on the mat,
Next to muddy paw prints left by the cat!

Coffee and cream, crushed into the coloured bedspread,
Sleek, shining magazines lying as if they are dead,
Spilt strawberry milkshake stained onto my books,
Go on I dare, you take a look!

Although my room is dirty,
I wouldn't swap it for a bag of pearls,
Though it's messy,
It's part of *my* world!

Lucy Moore (10)
Wigmore Primary School, Leominster

My Bedroom

When I walk in my room I can see . . .
Mouldy, muddy football boots,
Smashed PS2 games,
Bowls full of ice cream upside down on the floor,
Chocolate melted on the door handle,
Lots of teddies jumbled on the chair,
Toys stuffed under the bed,
Rubbish in a corner piled high like a mountain,
Rotting apple cores,
Dirty, dusty fingerprints on the TV
Pongy, smelly, stinky socks,
Spilt paint and toy cars scattered on the floor.
That's my room!

Jake Pontifex-Price (10)
Wigmore Primary School, Leominster

What A Messy Bedroom

What a messy bedroom my bedroom
I stand at my door and see this sea of messy untidy,
None can possibly be clean clothes.

My old, old, old footy boots, which my father adored
Resting in a very draughty corner.

Smelly socks galore all over the floor
Afraid of mothers none stinking washday!

My make-up box piled high to the brim
Exploding like a volcano
The red lipstick acting as lava
Hope the house does not tremble, I have no excuses this time.
It happened before said it will go away sometime.

Moti Alder (10)
Wigmore Primary School, Leominster

The Bedroom

As I open my bedroom door,
Squeak, squeak the floorboards
Under my dull, dingy carpet,
My clothes spill out of the wardrobe door.
Sticky sweets squished,
Squashed into my mucky carpet,
Smudged, smeary fingerprints on the PC screen.
PlayStation 2 games, books and CDs
Fighting for a place on the shelf.
Duvet drooping down from my cabin bed.
I swagger over the clutter.
Tick-tock! Tick-tock!
Sings my clock
Cars whizz at top speed,
Past my bedroom window,
My pool table is stained with green gunge.

Enter if you dare!

Jamie Bufton (10)
Wigmore Primary School, Leominster

What Am I?

Put in my key, tickle me with it, and then hear me roar into life.
Push my feet and look at me run.
My eyes glisten in the cool night air!
I'm searching for liquid food.
Wash me with soap,
Water splashing everywhere,
Suddenly, air is compressed against my body,
And I'm dry.

Turn the wheel and I will also turn.
Fill me up with oil so I can run on for longer,
Oil circulates my body.
Charging me up for the next time I run.

Hear my roar getting quieter and quieter,
Take out the key and I sleep.

Dominic Ryan (10)
Wigmore Primary School, Leominster

Filthy Bedroom

Scummy coffee in filthy cups,
Lego scattered on the floor,
Muddy paws made by collie pups,
Ripped up posters hanging off the wall,
Loads of packets from scattered 'McCoy's',
Cola cans found on unmade beds,
The whole room full of puddles of toys,
Pencil sharpenings and crumbs of bread,
Jabbed open cases, broken silver discs,
Ripped up paper in tiny bits,
All my friends take unknown risks,
I'm embarrassed more than a bit.

Harry Timmins (9)
Wigmore Primary School, Leominster

My Bedroom

I don't like my bedroom!
It's dressed in blue and purple with a little wooden bed.
It's a comfy little nest but it's far too gaudy!
There's a huge wardrobe that takes up all the space,
But not to worry,
It sometimes holds my clothes!

Little metal computer desk, resting in the corner,
White flickering computer screen,
Flumped on the computer desk.

Light brown patchwork chair,
Tucked under the computer desk.
Little wooden shelves, piled high with my wonderful books,
Cool CDs and special DVDs.

Molly Jones (9)
Wigmore Primary School, Leominster

My Bedroom

Smelly socks on the floor,
Bags piled high in the corner of the room.
The desk erupting with books and paper,
Teddies everywhere you look.
Something sticky on the floor,
Three dirty cups on the side.
Stains all over the sheets and on the pillows.
A dusty sink in the corner of the room,
Toys piled on top of a box.
My bedroom!

Rebecca Manuel (10)
Wigmore Primary School, Leominster

What Am I?

Put in my key, twist and let me start
I belch out dirty smoke
Eating up my passengers one by one
Travelling from place to place
My bright eyes shining
My stomach rumbles
As I stop I squeak horribly
As I start again there is more squeaking
I have ripped seats and dirty floor
Horrible dirty windows
I stop at the station to refill
I drink my diesel for my lunch
Then carry my passengers to where they want to go
And spit them out.

Greg Jones (11)
Wigmore Primary School, Leominster

Quad Bike

Put some oil in my hungry stomach.
Pull my lead let me go.
Then let go me. I blast through the air.
Dumps, jumps, rocks and rolls
Roars like a lion, screams like a girl.
Faster than a herd of sheep.
I round them up into their barn.
I tug my trailer full of hay to feed them.
Park me up for another day
Soon I'll be working
For you again.

Thomas Stevens (10)
Wigmore Primary School, Leominster

Football Match

F ootballs are for kicking not for throwing in the net
O ver the top bar goes the ball
O h no! it's raining heavy
T ackle the players, the ball is mine
B e careful, the other team will tackle too
A ngry, some parents with the ref
L ost the match but never mind
L et's try to win some other time.

Jack Galliers (8)
Wigmore Primary School, Leominster

What Am I?

Plush black interior
My eighteen inch rims shine against ship windows
My eyes smoked so you can't see in
My long, sleek, black body cruises gracefully along the seafront
My six arms open
Swallowing shiny discs to give you music.
Only the best champagne for my passengers
Flip down my screen and watch my five star entertainment
I roar ready to go.

Dale Willams (11)
Wigmore Primary School, Leominster

Mystery

You turn my key my brain switches on,
I can lift and pull anything,
The blood is pumped through my interior,
My eyes light up the dark night sky,
My lungs shake and pant as I pull, yank and
Heave my heavy loads,
I guzzle liquid food,
You take out the key I then sleep.

Harry Whiteman (11)
Wigmore Primary School, Leominster

What's Around Me?

Stuck in a car park, bored to rust!
Neon flashes everywhere,
The exhilaration pumping up inside me,
Maroon Mazda howling into the dark of the night,
Harpooning helicopters diving out of the sky,
Sundown is nigh,
Troublesome trains awaiting passengers,
Acrobatic aeroplanes flying overhead,
All the time in the world when I'm
Clamped!

Ben Timmins (10)
Wigmore Primary School, Leominster

What Am I?

My leg gets kicked again and again,
I roar to life.
My lights blind you as I zoom past.
My belly gets filled with liquid food.
I cough and throb as I'm left in a pitch-black space,
Burping out poisonous smoke,
Fast and faster, I speed.

Rhys Brown (11)
Wigmore Primary School, Leominster

What Am I?

My huge white arms stretch out by my side,
At night my many eyes glow all along my sleek side,
My round belly is filled with happy campers and their luggage,
My long, wide body glides through the mist,
My voice grumbles as I fly through the air,
My propeller spins violently, grasping the mist,
My nose leads the way all the way home.

Harriet Hodnett (10)
Wigmore Primary School, Leominster

The Race

Tickle the keys and watch me go,
Never caring where I travel
As long as it's the way I know.
I stand there with a tube down my side
Filling me up with energy so I can ride.
I zoom around corners
Away I go, beeping to the people I know.

Roaring like mad,
Get out of my way,
Because I really go fast
I'm like a jaguar catching its prey.
Zooming past all the other cold-blooded creatures.
Screeching around corners
Watch the sparks fly
I fly past the ribbon screaming with joy.
I've won.

Bethany Wooldridge (10)
Wigmore Primary School, Leominster

Scrambler Motorbike

Turn the key and roar to life,
Wheels cut through mud like a blunt knife.
Kicking muck up as the wheels spin round,
Choking out smoke with a banging sound
Wheel screeching
Fantastic, fast, furious
Shiny colours flash,
Quick and nimble, see me fly!
Only the best bike in the world.
Give it a try!

James Ruell (11)
Wigmore Primary School, Leominster

Who Am I?

Sitting in the corner of the kitchen I shake and hum,
Quick open my mouth.
I see your food and I am starving.
Open my enormous, snarling mouth
I will cool your food or
Open my gigantic, roaring stomach
And I will freeze your food.
My mouth holds; fruit smoothies,
Fromage frais,
Fruit and veg, all sorts of meats,
Ready meals
Drinks and my favourite . . . dairy products.
My stomach holds: ice cream, any foods you'd like to savour.
So I could do you a favour!
Now you can relax while I freeze
Or cool your food at low degrees!
Open my mouth, my light flickers off!
I have been here for years, shaking and humming
In the corner of the kitchen.
Still, I live on!

Abigail Poole (11)
Wigmore Primary School, Leominster

What Am I?

I suck the key through a slot,
My stomach grumbles and groans as I start work.
Wearing of my deep brown coat,
Smashing and crashing and bumping about.
Rolling around and taking off into the air,
Screeching and skidding round sharp corners,
Pushing off rivals to get to the top.
The winner!

James Phillips (10)
Wigmore Primary School, Leominster

What Am I?

I let out a mighty roar as I'm punctured by your key . . .
My round legs run speedily along the ground.
I swallow my prey whole.
I make a roaring rumbling sound.
During the night so dim and black, my eyes shine like the stars.
In the scariness of a storm, count on me to keep you warm.
As the rain peppers down, my wipers squeal and squeak.
I charge through the forest and roar through the green woods.
A black, stagnant liquid is fed through my side.
Take out my key, I'll rest till another day.

Rebecca Andrews (10)
Wigmore Primary School, Leominster

Night

Night is nasty and horrible as we never seem to understand him.
He creeps up on me and scares me,
Where does he live? What is he?

Night is a burglar who steals my family and friends,
He takes me to a place nobody knows.
I try to get out but he just stops me.
He makes me have horrible dreams.
He makes me feel lonely.

Night has eyes they shine like stars,
You can't see his face, it's hidden in the dark.
The clouds are his hair.
He has a dark black cloud
That fills the sky and makes it black.

Night lives behind the sun.
He only comes out when the sun is set.
He shocks me with fear.
I never have fun going to sleep,
Because I always know night is near.

Charles Thornton (10)
Woodfield Middle School, Redditch

Eagle

The eagle is the king of the sky.
Stalking his prey in the dawn of the day.
Fast as the wind, a piercing glare
Gives me a sudden scare.

The eagle has claws like razor blades,
One in the prey's back in this life fades.
His feathers are black, brown,
That camouflage in the trees.
A squawk from his beak
The creatures below all freeze.

If I was an eagle as still as a statue,
I'll say to the prey let me come and catch you.
With my talons so fierce,
And ready to pierce,
The creatures cry, death is quick, no time for tears.

Sophie Beer (11)
Woodfield Middle School, Redditch

Night

Night is kind and caring
Letting animals get away from the heat and brightness of the sun,
Night is a comforter hiding things,
That people don't want to see
And keeping me hidden from things
I don't want him to see me
Night is a hider, hiding in his house
In a pitch-black cave in enormous mountains.
Night is a caring grandpa
His star-like eyes keep watch over us.
Night is a traveller roaming the world, swiftly, silently undetected,
Night is a mother who covers the world and protect us,
Night is a mystery who we will never understand.

George West (11)
Woodfield Middle School, Redditch

My Hobby

I
Like
Pool it
Relaxes me,
When the red
And yellow balls
Fly in the pockets
And round the table.
I like the cue hitting
The white into the black
Left, right, forwards, backwards,
Side to side and round the outside.
I like pool when I beat my dad. I like
Pool plus I can't want to be in a professional
Team when I'm older. I like pool I
Was born to play, yes I was born to play this
Game!

Jake Moore (10)
Woodfield Middle School, Redditch

Night

Night may kill,
Kill our dreams.
Make us sad,
Make us scream.
Creeping upon us swiftly and unknowingly.
Scaring us all night.
We're safe in the morning,
Until . . .
The next night.
But yet again night will kill,
Kill our dreams.

Nomaan Jawed (11)
Woodfield Middle School, Redditch

Night

Night is kind like your mom and dad,
Night is comforting like the sand on the beach,
Night is safe.

Night makes me think of sweet dreams,
Night is caring like your grandma,
When you're in your bed night keeps you safe from harm.

Night has a comforting and sweet face,
She has small, soft eyes like a swimming pool,
She has red lips lined with lipstick.

She has sparkling white teeth like the stars in the sky,
She has spotty-coloured hair like spots on your pillow.

She moves slowly like the sun setting,
She lives up between the stars and the moon,
Night calms you down after a hard and exciting day.

Gabrielle Lewis (10)
Woodfield Middle School, Redditch

Night

Night is calm and generous
It surrounds us with its love
She gives us time for reflection
And supplies me with sweet dreams.

Her eyes are like two crystal balls
Quite beautiful in herself
She lives above on a heap of clouds
To check on me all night.

It's like a mother with her baby
Surrounding me with happiness
But when I wake, I just can't wait
To get back home again.

Mia Whittaker (11)
Woodfield Middle School, Redditch

Eagle

The eagle is a horrid hunter
Just standing there, eyeing up his innocent victims,
That would soon be his prey.

The eagle, the king of the sky,
Clutching the eye of the mountains,
Letting them crumble and rumble
As he lets out a threatening and very much deafening sound.

The eagle's razor blade claws
Pecking out and then
All of a sudden . . .

There he is, there and back for this predator can't hold back,
He swoops like a kite and flies like a bat
For when they turn, they never turn back.

And still he sits on the edge of the crag,
Waiting to make his move on another poor and helpless creature.

Laura Spurrier (11)
Woodfield Middle School, Redditch

Night

Night can be friendly giving you sweet dreams,
Night can be hellish giving you nightmares.

He lives in the mountains, touching the sky,
He creeps up in the daytime making it night.

I met him once in his land of dreams,
He was wearing pyjamas with constellations on them.

Night turned my dream into a nightmare
And trapped me in.
I asked him to leave me,
So he gave me a sweet dream.

Jack Shakles (11)
Woodfield Middle School, Redditch

Night

Night is nasty like an evil witch,
Night is as spooky as a monster,
Night makes you lonely,
Because night has its own atmosphere,
Night makes you think of spooky nightmares,
Like if ghosts are coming to get you,
Night is a burglar that steals my family,
Night causes you to think you live on the road,
Night has a face like a ghost,
His eyes are bright green, his mouth is tiny
And has lips that are black and white,
Night has bright yellow hair, he wears a spooky cloak,
Night moves as quiet as a ghost,
Night might live behind the sun,
He wakes me and makes my cry.

Iqra Ali (11)
Woodfield Middle School, Redditch

Night

She is dark and nasty
But kind in some way.
She steals your dreams like a burglar
Stealing some precious jewels.
She is lonely but safe,
Wraps her arms around you, you feel her
You try to drift off and have happy dreams
But somehow turn into horrible nightmares,
You wake up and come face to face with . . .
Thick, greasy, long locks with eyes like deep pools of gleaming oil,
Clothes like kitchen oil and covered in pure *evil!*

Paige Preece (11)
Woodfield Middle School, Redditch

Night

It creeps through the sky,
And into your house,
Sprinkled stars spy,
Like a thousand eyes.

He is night.

He spreads into every corner,
Wedged between books,
Until you see nothing,
A time favoured by crooks.

He is night.

Darkness surrounds you,
Unable to see,
While he hoots and whoops,
Telling you to flee.

He is night.

Soon it will be morning,
Remember the light,
Playing, laughing and jumping
Before we know, again it will be night.

Chloe Laight (11)
Woodfield Middle School, Redditch

Night

Night is as dull as a bat's wings,
Creeping towards you from the middle of a deep forest,
He moves swiftly and fast as if he wants to get you.

He is creepy and black like the night sky,
With only a twinkle of light to guide your way.
He screams and shouts, kicks and bangs,
Night is after you!

Melissa Mogg (10)
Woodfield Middle School, Redditch

Night

She is kind and caring,
Controlling your dreams.
She is a guardian angel watching over you and me.
Her nylon hair keeps us warm,
Like a blanket on a cold winter's night.
She wears a burgundy silk dress
Pretty in the moonlight.
The tiara on her soft silky hair is shiny and glossy.
She fights the sun into his bed,
So he can rest his weary head.
With her wings most beautiful,
I beg of thee,
She is not my enemy.
She is my angel, my guardian.
Your dreams are her doing.
Don't mess with fate.
She will give you dreams for the
Rest of your days.

Errin Smith (11)
Woodfield Middle School, Redditch

Eagles

Eagles devour their prey all night and all day
Eagles live up high and they're king of the sky
Eagles sit and wait for days with their claws like razor blades
They swoop down as fast as the speed of light,
Sometimes day, sometimes night.
They fly around elegantly, trying to move peacefully,
Eagles are so big they can't stay on a twig.
They have a beak like a knife, ready to protect its children and wife.

Adam McIlravey (10)
Woodfield Middle School, Redditch

I . . .

Today I have this room,
Not forever but for this lesson.
Today I have this pen with clear blue ink,
And I am no friend shorter.
How well I write with it unlike her.

And yesterday I had the house,
The kitchen and the telly.
Yesterday I had the time,
The time to think and be alone.
How good it felt,
And I would not have done anything else.

And tomorrow I will have my violin,
Not completely mine but for this term.
Perfect for practising and people to hear.
I will have myself, all alone.

Rosie Irwin (11)
Woodfield Middle School, Redditch

Eagle

The feathered king sat perched in the tree
Amongst the beautiful landscape,
His dark beady eyes show no life,
But we know he is waiting, watching the feast below,
He spreads his wings to full capacity and swoops with such precision,
His mighty talons taking hold of his first course.
Slightly satisfied he returns to his watch tower to begin his search again.

Harry Bishop (10)
Woodfield Middle School, Redditch

Night

Night is friendly,
She gives you happy dreams,
Comforting you and me to sleep cheerfully,
She gets lonely at midnight when she has tucked everybody
To sleep,
Night is like a loving mother giving the sun a rest.

She has got an old pale wrinkly face,
Her eyes are scrunched into her soft face,
She has lips which are pale blue with miniature cracks in,
Her wonderful wavy hair snuggles you in bed peacefully,
Night's clothes are just plain baby blue with a dark blue cape
Covering the sky,

She plods around every house to check you and me are having
A good night's sleep!

Charlotte Gregg (10)
Woodfield Middle School, Redditch

Night

He summons himself from the darkness
Swiftly he moves down the solitary streets
His crude smile strikes terror into whoever sets eyes upon him
His deep black eyes are like pools of darkness
He steals your dreams and turns them into vast, unescapable
nightmares

His long grey coats flutter in the wind
Whilst his black hood covers his evil, repulsive face
One look could obliterate your happiness.

But upon dawn he vanishes and when you wake up
You hope you don't ever feel him trespassing
In your mind like a deadly parasite ever again.

Adam Coles (10)
Woodfield Middle School, Redditch

The Moon

The moon is kind not nasty
Gives you dreams not ghastly nightmares
A caring person like a caring mother
Sends you hugs when you are sleeping
Blows you kisses when you are weeping
Helps you sleep
Till day is near
With beautiful soft lips
That smiles and laughs
And crystal-blue eyes
Beaming down upon thee
With a navy blue dress
Flowing in the night wind
With the stars that she shines
Are above us
Twinkling way up high
The moon is kind and caring
And waves us all goodbye.

Heather Minihane (11)
Woodfield Middle School, Redditch

Eagle

Eagles are the kings of the sky
They fly and fly way up high.

Their soft, white feathers blow in the wind,
As they move gracefully through the sky.

Their claws are as sharp as razors,
Their eyes are as red as hot coals.

Their elegant feet prowl round their prey
And sink their teeth low into it!

Eagles are extraordinary creatures
And hopefully they won't be extinct.

Ellie Taylor (10)
Woodfield Middle School, Redditch

Night

His scarred face is pale,
Knowing his guilt, his crime,
Stealing the day causes his dilemma,
How long can he hide?

His eyes are as brown as mouth-watering chocolate,
Which camouflages him when he prowls around the city,
Searching for a spot to hide from the police,
As he is on the run from the law!

His robes are draped over him like a sea of blackness,
Making him blend in with the shadows,
Helpful with his mysterious spy work,
Useful for his hiding.

Even though he can never be captured,
A punishment still finds him,
The sun washes him away like a sandcastle on a beach,
Every morning, for all eternity!

Louise Harris (10)
Woodfield Middle School, Redditch

Night

He's coming, I know it
He's nearly here to frighten, to scare, so beware.
His eyes all beady and red with oil-black pupils.
His mouth all crusty, scabby and dry.
I can smell the stench of his grease and mould.
There in the doorway, his eyes gleaming,
All I can hear is stomping, now I'm trapped!

Now all my thoughts are nightmares and pain.
It's torture, it's torture, oh please go away.
The sun starts to rise, it's morning now
But I've not escaped, oh no!
He'll feed on me again
So all I can do is wait . . .

Kaya Hodgkins (11)
Woodfield Middle School, Redditch

Night

Night will come taking away all bad dreams,
A chance to relax and take a walk in the park,
She looks you in the eye with all her kindness
Like a mother with her children.

She moves swiftly in the night sky,
Her eyes shaped as sparkly stars,
Her hair very dark and long
Her face, dark, pretty and kind looking.

She is very lonely and safe
Comforting everybody,
Making every person happy,
So now it's time to say goodnight!
'Goodnight.'

Melissa Keen (11)
Woodfield Middle School, Redditch

Night

Night is kind and caring,
Swaying from house to house.
Comforting children,
Sending them all pleasant sweet dreams.
She flies through the sky,
Leaving a trail of glistening shiny stars.
With her round soothing face,
She keeps everyone safe.
Watching over them in their beds,
Singing them to sleep.
Her half-shut smiling eyes and long thin mouth.
People always look up to her,
Until she fades away.
Ready for night to follow after day.

Emily Critchlow (11)
Woodfield Middle School, Redditch

My Hobby

My hobby is horses,
Horses I do like,
They sometimes dance,
They sometimes prance,
And sometimes jump through smoke.
Horses are my hobby,
Horses are my life,
Sometimes they are fussy,
Sometimes they are great,
The only one thing that horses hate,
Is when you don't give them bait,
So horses are my hobby, my most favourite hobby.

Lucy Prudden (11)
Woodfield Middle School, Redditch

Young Writers Information

We hope you have enjoyed reading this book - and that you will continue to enjoy it in the coming years.

If you like reading and writing poetry drop us a line, or give us a call, and we'll send you a free information pack.

Alternatively if you would like to order further copies of this book or any of our other titles, then please give us a call or log onto our website at www.youngwriters.co.uk

Young Writers Information
Remus House
Coltsfoot Drive
Peterborough
PE2 9JX

(01733) 890066